The Glass Cliff

The Glass Cliff

One Transman's Leadership Odyssey

Mel Rutherford, PhD

Library of Congress Cataloging-in-Publication Data Applied for:

Paperback ISBN: 978-1-394-36867-9
ePDF: 978-1-394-36869-3
ePub: 978-1-394-36868-6

Cover Design: Wiley
Cover Image: © erhui1979/Getty Images

Set in 9.5/12.5pt STIXTwoText by Straive, Pondicherry, India

SKY5D41C6CA-F733-416D-A168-7D499F891312_042426

Contents

Preface

This is my story about leading an academic department during troubled times. I was given my first real leadership opportunity when my department was in crisis. I read leadership books and took leadership courses, but the guidance I found available was about growth, expansion, change, or profit. It was not tailored to leading in a crisis. My experience was confusing, rewarding, painful, and meaningful. One of the most surprising parts was my ability to succeed in my department and to have real wins while my relationship with the administration that hired me struggled. As I leaned on my values to guide me, my journey was bewildering: I experienced breakthroughs and accolades in my department, but condemnation from above.

I wanted to share both my story and what I learned about leadership on the way. Some of my challenges were unique to my gender, like the reprisal I faced after being misgendered, but some would have been barriers for anyone who accepted my particular leadership challenge. I wrote this book to share with you the strategies I tried, the approaches that I thought were useful for leading during a crisis, my thoughts on making leadership accessible to transgender and nonbinary leaders, and the lessons I learned along the way. I hope my story will be useful for you if you are leading during troubled times.

Author's Note

In exchanges with the president, The Administrator, The Supervisor, and Human Resources, anything that appears in quote marks is taken directly from emails, documents, or audio recordings of conversations. Those quotes have been edited only to remove proper names.

1

The Crisis and the Calling

On Friday April 16, 2021, Ontario's Premier, Doug Ford, announced a strict shutdown as COVID-19 cases were spiking once again. Schools were closed. Stores were closed. Gyms, playgrounds, golf courses, and places of worship were all shuttered. Funerals were limited to ten mourners. No one could enter anyone else's home, and even outdoor gatherings with people from different households were banned.

Stay-at-home orders were expected to last six weeks, enforced with new powers: police could ask anyone outside of their homes to provide their address and their reason for being out, with fines of $750 for unsatisfactory answers. The Ontario Provincial Police planned to screen all vehicles crossing into the province starting on Monday, one minute after midnight.

That night at dinner, my wife Melanie asked my two teenagers, Emerson and Xander, if they wanted to leave the province. Our kids are both competitive swimmers. They were allowed to train during shutdowns, but no pools were open nearby, and their training was stalled. School was online, so they lay in bed during class, cameras and microphones off. Social isolation pressed down hard. They decided to go where they could swim.

At dawn the next morning, Melanie, Emerson, and Xander drove out of the driveway, the car loaded with clothes, swim gear, and Xander's desktop computer. They were off on their 30-hour drive to New Mexico to stay with Melanie's father—racing the clock before new travel restrictions took effect.

For the next three and a half months, I was home alone—forbidden from seeing anyone and leaving my house only for solo hikes. Restaurants were closed. Trips to the grocery store invited suspicion. I dove deep into our freezer, surviving on a bizarre selection of forgotten meals, some good, some freezer-burned, and some just plain inscrutable. Before my family returned, I had posted my new strongly worded "freezer rules" on the fridge.

Freezer Rules

Do you put food in the freezer that you never intend to retrieve?

No.

Do you put food in the freezer with no date, so no one will know how old it is?

No.

Do you put food in the freezer with no label, so no one will know what kind of food it is?

No.

Do you put food in the freezer that is not properly packaged, leaving it to get freezer burn?

No.

Do you put food in the freezer that no one will ever eat?

No.

With plenty of time on my hands, I was prepared to offer feedback on their use of the freezer.

Isolation was wild and disorienting. Work meetings and social connections were flattened onto two-dimensional Zoom squares. I sat in my chair in the living room each Sunday watching the minister of my local Unitarian Universalist church deliver her sermon on Zoom. As an introvert, I thought I'd be fine, but sixteen weeks of solitude was a test.

I learned the Star Trek: Voyager theme on my French horn, practiced scales on my bass guitar, and explored the local hiking trails that I'd never found in twenty years of living in my house. I binge-watched Ozark and Orange is the New Black, and I slept a lot. My only companions were my two dogs, Khalo, a dachshund, and Zia, a blue healer mix, with whom I developed routines. We went on daily morning walks, cautiously keeping our distance from any humans we encountered. In the afternoon, I'd throw a stick in the front yard until somebody wandered off to chew on it. Every evening, I let them know it was bedtime by singing the bedtime song. The experience was surreal and exhausting. Eventually I lost track of what day it was. How long had I been alone?

It was during this period of isolation that I became my university's first transgender department chair.

Department Interrupted

While the world was gripped by a global pandemic, my academic department was facing its own crisis. On February 19, 2020, just eight days after the World Health Organization named the new virus COVID-19, our department received an email from our dean telling us that "a faculty member has been suspended." The email went on to say that "undergraduate courses have been reassigned and we will work with individual graduate students to ensure their progress is not interrupted." Despite this promise, the entire department was interrupted.

That first email from the dean signaled the beginning of a series of escalating events. By August, dozens of allegations had been made under the sexual violence and the sexual harassment policies against seven current and former department members. The accused were faculty, staff, and a student. They were queer and straight. Three of the current members of our department who were accused were men. People were barred from campus, and subsequently investigated, before eventually being reintegrated into the department. Each new allegation was publicly announced, igniting the exuberance of the local media, who reported on the story as if a sex ring had been exposed and brought to justice.

I was dumbfounded. With every new announcement, I struggled to make sense of what I was hearing. How could it be that so many people in my department had been engaged in wrongdoing without my knowing? Early in the months of turmoil, my graduate students came to my office to ask me if I had heard the news. I had no insider information to offer them. They speculated about who it might be who had been "suspended," but they were unable to guess.

The accused individuals were not allowed to speak to each other or to anyone else in the university community as they waited to hear what their accusations were. Then they waited some more. We all waited. It took eight months before everyone knew what they were accused of. They were perplexed. We were all disoriented. Posters were circulated with the photograph and name of people who had been accused, instructing anyone who saw these people on campus to call security. Care was taken to ensure that anyone who worked with or knew the accused saw the posters. One of the accused needed to ask for special permission to take her child to the campus hospital for a medical appointment.

In July of 2020, as allegations were accumulating, the university's president announced that he had ordered a "systemic review" of our department, a euphemism for an investigation, "to determine whether there existed systemic or cultural issues within the department that need to be surfaced and addressed." The introduction to the survey that people took stated that the investigator would "provide expert advice and guidance on the options that are available to improve the culture of the department," strongly suggesting that the department's culture needed improvement.

These events were tremendously disruptive to the department's teaching, to our research, and to our community. While the accused were put on involuntary leaves for up to eight months pending the investigations, new supervisors had to be found for eleven graduate students and dozens of undergraduate thesis students. In our department, as in most science departments, student training uses an apprenticeship model. It was not a simple task to reassign a student to a different faculty mentor because each student had already invested months or years in developing a research program in their supervisor's area of expertise. The new faculty supervisors who were drafted to rescue the stranded students were not necessarily familiar with the students' research. One student was reassigned to a mentor in a different department, and she ultimately quit the program rather than learn a whole new discipline. One student finished the program with supervisors in a different country. The undergraduate thesis students never saw their supervisors again.

Three former graduate students were unable to work with their supervisors to publish research data that they had already collected. In academia, publications are the currency—the deliverable for which someone's work is recognized. To invest years in a research project and then be unable to publish it is a substantial disappointment. Some students were unable to get letters of recommendation, a necessity for professional advancement in academia. An application that does not include a letter from one's supervisor is viewed with suspicion. Twenty-seven graduate students had to replace members of their supervisory committees—the small advisory group that oversees a graduate student's progress. This disruption meant a loss of expertise, a loss of relationships, and significant delay. We had a record number of undergraduate classes taught by contract instructors, some of whom were hired in the middle of an on-going course. Some undergraduate courses were not delivered.

Our department's community was deeply impacted. The months-long publicity while the investigations were being organized and conducted interrupted the comfortable relationships between graduate students and their supervisors. Trust was replaced by mistrust. After months of confusion, I had a virtual lab meeting to talk to my own graduate students. They were baffled by what was happening and having trouble making progress with their work.

Because we were working remotely, there were no serendipitous water cooler conversations. The accusations, the publicity, the investigations, and the eventual reintegration of the accused happened when we were not gathering in person, so the usual easy access to compassion and support was thwarted. Nearly everyone in the department was confounded by what we were reading in the newspapers. We are a tight-knit department, with about 30 faculty members and about 110 graduate students. We desperately needed to talk with one another, but we were stuck at home.

About now, you may be dying to know what happened that had led to this torrent of accusations. You might even feel frustrated with this lack of clarity. That is how I felt. We were all in the same boat. The lack of information was deafening.

A Dangerous Promotion

In the midst of both local and global turmoil, our department chair's five-year term was coming to an end, and we needed to select a new leader. Nobody wanted the job given the circumstances. While the role of chair has its perks, including a research stipend, teaching release, and a really nice office with a view of the entire campus, this promotion was clearly a hornet's nest. Helping people within the department reorient to work after the disruption was going to be a challenge, and relationships with the university's upper administration had been strained for months. While the chair position is considered a promotion, it was clear that this was no path to greater leadership opportunities.

What the new chair would be stepping into was not entirely clear. We were confused. I didn't understand how this unprecedented volume of allegations had come about. The university's administration was sharing no information with the department leadership that would help anyone who was considering taking the position. It was clear that the job of leading this department was daunting. It was not clear what support was on offer from the administration, if any.

Many members of our department felt unseen and misunderstood. Because the allegations against members of our department had been widely publicized and because the department itself had been publicly scrutinized, we did not feel like the years that we had spent creating a collaborative, student-centered culture was being recognized or appreciated. The department that was being portrayed in the local media did not sound like the department we knew. It was disappointing and frustrating to feel so unheard. It hurt.

Following the president's announcement that the whole department was under investigation, communication with the university's leaders chilled, and we no longer found it possible to voice our concerns about what was happening. Information about what concerns had triggered an investigation into our department continued to be difficult to find. Communication and collaboration became impossible. I was left to make inferences based on what I had read in the news.

When I heard in 2020 that there would be a "systemic review" of our department's culture, I wasn't initially worried. If any department was going to ace the culture test, it was ours. I was naïve. The investigation into the department's culture yielded no finding of facts, but in December of 2020, the president publicly announced his own conclusions from this investigation. The president declared that our department had systemic and cultural issues, which have "created a degree of complacency that has let inappropriate behaviours go unchecked." It was strange that the systemic review preceded the individual investigations. The president announced how the systemic review explained the inappropriate behavior before the investigations of the allegations revealed whether there was any inappropriate behavior to be explained.

The moment I read the president's characterization of the department's complacency, I thought no one was going to want to chair the department. Without naming names, the president was implying that the department leadership was responsible for these events that had so deeply impacted our operations. Who else would it be who had "let inappropriate behaviours go unchecked"? The reputation of the entire department was tarnished. The years of work we had put into building a supportive culture was dismissed. Once the investigations were complete and people had returned to work, the president didn't rescind his statement about our complacency for nearly four years.

The statement by the university president made the position of department chair perilous. When the chair of Dartmouth University's psychology department was publicly accused of "looking the other way," when complaints were surfacing in his department, he ended his life at the age of 50. Like ours, his department had drawn substantial publicity after a number of graduate students alleged sexual harassment, assault, and misconduct. Students alleged that Dartmouth had ignored or mishandled early reports. The department chair wanted to publicly disavow the claim that he had looked the other way, but the university advised him to hold his tongue. He never felt vindicated, and he became depressed. Our president's announcement impacted our department's reputation and the reputation of the department's leadership and consequently impacted our chances of finding a new chair. It could be ruinous to anyone's reputation to become the next chair of a department accused of complacency. This would be a high-risk promotion.

As the search for our next department chair began, I knew I didn't want the job, so I ran for election to the chair selection committee. I thought serving on the selection committee was a productive way to help my department, and also a good place to sit out the storm. I was elected, and therefore ineligible for the role of chair according to policy.

The selection committee was chaired by our dean, a cardiovascular physiologist, who had known me since our children went to the same on-campus childcare center over 15 years prior. At the childcare center, she had chaired the parent's group, and Melanie and I had worked with her in that capacity. When she became dean in 2017, I went to a welcome mixer that she hosted as the first woman to serve as dean of science.

From my vantage point on the chair selection committee, I watched the selection process become dire. Due to the chaos in the department, we had begun the selection process many months later than would have been ideal. Still, it felt like we were taking our time to go through the motions of a possibly futile search process. Each committee member reached out to their constituents to hear what they thought we were looking for in a chair. Documents were circulated listing the opportunities and challenges the new chair would be inheriting. This information would have been useful if we had had a list of candidates to choose from, but no one applied.

The dean escalated her search. She asked a number of my colleagues if they were interested in the position. They were not. Some of them told me about the incentives she was offering: teaching release, a research allowance, and a year-long administrative leave at the end of the term. Still, she got a firm "no" from each of them. Filling this role seemed impossible. The challenge of getting the confused, demoralized department back to work was daunting. Being visibly associated with such a besmirched department seemed like a poor choice for someone with aspirations to a higher leadership position in the university. The department was in desperate need of a leader who could steer everyone through the painful epoch we were in. We had no candidates. We were running out of time.

Our chair selection committee had no one to select.

Could We Be Looking for Me?

Part of my job as a member of the selection committee was to reach out to my colleagues to ask for nominations. As I canvassed my colleagues for suggestions, several faculty members and students suggested that I would be a good chair. They told me that although I was quiet, I was seen as compassionate. They told me that I was known to be a good listener, and they thought that I would be fair. One colleague told me that I was providing a positive role model for work-life balance by making my parenting so conspicuous. More than one commented that as a transman I would be able to understand numerous perspectives and bring a greater sense of inclusivity to the role. I was curious about whether my lived experience would offer a helpful perspective that would help me navigate the complexities of the disruption our department was experiencing.

I was an unlikely candidate. No one, me included, expected that I had leadership in my future. I had spent 20 years attending faculty meetings and saying next to nothing. I am quiet, I am introverted, and I generally only speak up when I think I have something to contribute. I was the 13th most senior faculty member in my department of 30.

I have been an academic all of my adult life, but I never planned on leadership being my path. I was dedicated to conducting research, mentoring my graduate students, and doing my best to deliver impactful teaching in the classroom. I earned my bachelor's degree in psychology from Yale University in 1992 and later went to the University of California, Santa Barbara, to study evolutionary psychology with Leda Cosmides and John Tooby, two of the scientists who founded the field. I earned my PhD in 2000, and after a two-year postdoctoral fellowship at the University of Denver, I accepted a permanent faculty position and moved to Canada. Melanie came with me. Little did she know the adventures we were in for.

I have a research lab studying social perception and its development. Some of my research involves babies looking at pictures of animals while we measure where they are looking, and some of my research measures differences in how adults perceive faces depending on whether we provide social category labels. I study whether an infant's and an adult's attention is captured by objects that would have been important to survival in our evolutionary history. Most years I have three or four graduate students in my lab, and sometimes I have a postdoctoral fellow as well.

I did have some leadership training and experience. As head of a dynamic research laboratory, I was engaged in leadership. I had served my department for one year as associate chair for graduate studies. In an attempt to develop my own leadership skills, I had recently enrolled in an online course called "Leadership Essentials," which I still regard as the best, most practical leadership course I've taken.

Was I the leader that our committee was searching for?

Bringing My Values to Work

As the chair "selection" committee was running out of time, I came to wonder whether I should chair the department. Until my department was impacted by the events of 2020, I had not considered how my personal values were relevant to my professional life. Work was where I taught and got research done, following the scientific training that I learned during my undergraduate and graduate education. My values, my community, and my impact on the world had nothing to do with work. Sure, I thought about freedom of expression, and evidence-based approaches to problems while at work, but I didn't think about whether my personal values impacted what I did at work. I hadn't thought about bringing my values into leadership.

It was in my Unitarian Universalist (UU) church community where I became familiar with values-based leadership—the approach that would ultimately guide me through my time as department chair. In North America, Unitarian Universalism is a liberal religion, characterized by a commitment to inclusivity. There is not a common creed other than a commitment to social justice and a commitment to being inclusive of theological diversity. I was raised in this religious tradition, after my parents discovered the First Unitarian Society of Salem, Oregon, when I was two years old.

Most of my leadership training and experience and the values that now underpin my leadership came from this community. More than a decade previously,

Gail, a wise elder in our church, asked me to participate in the Canadian Unitarian Universalist Leadership School. She had identified me as someone with leadership potential. She thought that both the church and I would benefit if I had some formal leadership training.

The students in this three-day course were members of my church and of several nearby UU churches. Coincidentally, we stayed in the dormitory facilities of the university where I work, and our learning took place on campus. We participated in creative workshops each day, ate our meals together, and made music and played board games in the evening. We learned about leaders taking care of congregants and leaders taking care of themselves. On our last day at the overnight camp, we worked together to create a service. It was an unusual opportunity to learn how Unitarian Universalists approach leadership and to spend some time with members of nearby congregations.

One of the illuminating stories that I heard at this leadership program was the tale of a woman who had to get up early every morning because she was in charge of making the sun rise. She had a ritual that she performed, and every time she did so, the sun came over the horizon to start the day. For many years she was happy to have this task. She was proud of how diligent and reliable she was, and she was pleased with how impactful her work was: her ritual was always followed by the sun rising. But as she aged, she got tired. She began searching for someone to replace her. Nobody wanted such a rigid job. She persisted in her daily task, now with less relish and eventually with a bit of resentment, until the morning came when she was finally unable to get up and summon the sun. To her surprise, the sun came up anyway.

This tale was a lesson in self-care. The leadership lesson was you don't have to do everything. If you are finding leadership exhausting and unrewarding, step back. If it is important enough, someone else will step up. If no one in the community steps up to adopt the task, that is okay too. Our department had arrived at that moment when our leader was spent. I thought about whether the call for new leadership was compelling enough for me to accept the responsibility.

Given the pain, trauma, and confusion we were experiencing, it appeared to me that our department needed someone to lead with compassion. People needed compassion in order to process what had happened to our department. Our graduate students had been separated from their supervisors, and their research had been interrupted. Students' academic progress had been disrupted. Lives had been disrupted. Some people had been even more intimately impacted. This group needed a leader who would be gentle when managing university processes, when trying to reintegrate people who were being returned to work, and when trying to guide the department as a whole back to the work that is our primary mission.

The second of the eight principles of Unitarian Universalism is "Justice, equity, and compassion in human relations." A compassionate leader for our department was going to need to provide information to quell the shock and confusion. The lack of clarity about what was happening and what we should be doing was painful for everyone. A compassionate leader was going to need to make time to listen to people. People needed to tell their stories and share what they had been experiencing. The department did not need a dictatorial or corrective boss. We needed a leader who could build trust and relationships to guide us out of this crisis. In my department, there are 200 people, if you count faculty, staff, postdocs, and grad students. If you count undergraduates there are about 1300 more. Every one of them deserves compassion.

Unitarian Universalists also value evidence. The fourth of the eight principles endorses "A free and responsible search for truth and meaning." This value is tailor-made for an academic department because research and discovery are our main mission. An evidence-based approach was just what our department needed. I have recently developed a graduate course in evidence-based approaches to diversity and inclusion. By teaching this course, I wanted to empower my students with the perspective that questions about attitudes, stereotypes, and prejudice are answerable, and I wanted to lay the foundations for a more gender-inclusive view of leadership.

In this course, we examined questions like to what extent do implicit biases predict real-world behavior? We read the literature, and although we didn't find the cure for prejudice in the published literature, we focused on the premise that the question can be studied. There is a lot of research on implicit biases that reveals that each of us has race-based and gender-based biases (Devine, 1989; Fazio et al., 1986; Greenwald & Banaji, 1995). Important questions remain, like what is the link between individual biases and systemic and institutional inequities? Are biases so baked into institutional practices and policies that they are insurmountable? What approaches to increasing inclusivity would be effective? In the course, we agreed that an evidence-based approach to dismantling transphobia and other oppressions is more likely to be successful than an intuition-based approach, and this conclusion is consistent with the responsible search for truth that is espoused by UU principles. We haven't solved racism, sexism, and transphobia yet, but as scientists, as psychologists, we do have tools in our professional tool kit that are relevant. We need to understand how the human mind works in order to advance our inclusive values.

My department also required integrity and required information that would allow them to draw their own conclusions about what had happened. The public characterization of our department did not match our view of who we were, a supportive, inclusive department. Our department is full of world-renowned scientists. It was clear to us that the president's systemic review lacked rigorous methods and scientific integrity. The questions were nebulous and biased and there was no comparison data. The systemic review could not yield interpretable results. In this context, leading with integrity meant slowing down when there was not enough information available to draw actionable conclusions.

The value of inclusion relates to the 3rd principle in Unitarian Universalism: "Acceptance of one another." I learned this from my UU teachings, and also from Melanie. Melanie is so inclusive that our parties are huge. At the time of their fifth birthday party, our twins were in preschool in the morning and kindergarten in the afternoon. We invited every kid in both of those classes to the party. Forty-four kids came, and each brought two presents. Of course they did. We had twins. Knee-deep in toys, our house was delightful chaos following that event. Similarly, when we got married, Melanie thought every kid should be invited to be the flower bearer, so our wedding party featured 36 children who each handed me a flower. These flowers became the bridal bouquet.

When we meet in my congregation, we say "Whoever you are, whomever you love, wherever you are in your journey of faith, you are the people of this church, and you are welcome here." My department needed to hear this message. They needed to know they were all welcome. When I convene a large gathering at work, I used these words of welcome, adapted for a secular community: "Whoever you are, wherever you're from, whomever you love, you are welcome here."

A persistent challenge in academic leadership is incorporating the perspectives of multiple stakeholders in decisions that impact them. This is relevant to the Unitarian Universalist's 5th principle, "The right of conscience and the use of the democratic process." Unitarian Universalists value both "the freedom of the pulpit" and "the freedom of the pew." The former suggests that the speaker in the pulpit is free to decide on the topic and offer their own opinions and beliefs. The freedom of the pew is less widely known. The listener, the audience, and the congregation in the pews have the right to their own free and responsible search for truth and meaning, even as they listen to the sage on the stage. From the pew, the listener can disbelieve, reanalyze, and reinterpret. The listener may be unpersuaded. The listener may disagree. The freedom of the pew is an invitation to critical thinking. One thing that I really like about both my religious community and my department is that we can care for people with whom we disagree, and we can include people with lots of different perspectives into our community.

Listening to and understanding other viewpoints and incorporating them into decision-making leads to more robust and equitable solutions than stifling discussion. It was in the context of my UU community that I learned about and began to practice formal consensus decision-making. In formal consensus decision-making, a proposal is not adopted until the group moves through a process designed to make space for all concerns to be considered. The priority is to hear every voice so that the final decision can incorporate all of the perspectives. Currently I am sitting on an advisory committee of the Canadian Unitarian Council that is trying to review best practices in decision-making. Formal consensus decision-making is one of the methods we are considering, and the one that I am tasked with presenting to the group.

In a recent meeting of the advisory committee, I explained the values: hearing every voice, tapping the creativity in the group, building a robust decision, and ending with a decision that has everyone's buy-in. I explained that decision-making proceeds by first understanding the proposal, then listening for concerns, then addressing the concerns, building a creative solution that incorporates all perspectives, and then carefully and slowly listening for consensus. I find formal consensus decision-making to be powerful, compassionate, fair, and equitable; I wondered if this deep listening would help our department's healing process.

Fundamental to leadership is the ability to build relationships with all of the people under your care. Unitarian Universalists value relationships both between individuals and across the community as a whole. The 8th principle says: "We affirm and promote individual and communal action that accountably dismantles racism and systemic barriers to full inclusion in ourselves and our institutions." Our department includes people of numerous and overlapping social categories, including many ethnicities, genders, places of origin, and religious backgrounds. A leader who keeps the importance of relationship building in mind could help build this community.

My leadership training and experience in the context of my UU community also introduced me to the idea of naming your values explicitly. Once your organization has named its values, those values can become the foundation of consensus decision-making. In the UU community, these values are the foundation of values-based leadership. During this time of crisis in our department, perhaps a values-based approach to leadership and to governance could be the answer.

Answering the Call

It was April 21, 2021, and here we sat, on another Zoom meeting of the chair selection committee. We looked like the tick-tack-toe grid from the opening credits of the Brady Bunch. We had completed the weeks-long process of defining our vision of the role, but we had no applicants. It was starting to look like we were wasting our time. I knew that my dean had had a very difficult time over the past year, and I knew she was working hard to find someone to chair this department. I wanted to help her.

It came to me as an epiphany.

The second it occurred to me that I was the right person to serve our department as chair, nothing else made sense. I felt called. I could do this job. I could take what I'd learned from Unitarian Universalism and from my experience as a transman and bring something unique to the role, bridging viewpoints and providing a role model.

My values could be the foundation of my leadership. I had worked for social justice my whole life, so I thought I was tough enough to endure whatever was to come.

As a transman, it was possible that I had happened into the only leadership opportunity that I would ever be offered. The Glass Cliff theory describes how minority leaders are often offered leadership roles during crises when the chances of their success are slim, a phenomenon linked to systemic biases (Ryan & Haslam, 2005). Straight, white, cisgender men may not consider a precarious leadership position because they are confident that there will be other, more propitious leadership opportunities available to them. Members of minority groups are not so confident that other leadership positions will come their way.

It was also possible that, as a transman, I had something to offer. Colonel Bree Fram is an astronautical engineer in the military and, until Trump's purge of trans troops, was one of the highest-ranking transgender leaders in the United States military. In their book *Forging Queer Leaders*, Fram and Cavallaro (2024) posit that transgender people have some special gifts, superpowers even, that are relevant to leadership.

Transgender people have chosen their own path and have done so in the face of societal objections. Trans leaders are people who have made the conscious choice to continue their work despite massive obstacles. Fram and Cavallaro point to coming out and discrimination as "crucible" experiences that make people both tougher and more empathetic.

> Whether it is finding the motivation to continue despite the exhaustion of dealing with constant marginalization or summoning the resilience to get back up after being knocked down, these leaders somehow find the energy to keep going. Further, they transform these experiences into enhanced capacities that make them better leaders and allow them to support others.
>
> *(Fram & Cavallaro, 2024, p. 155)*

Fram and Cavallaro suggest that the empathy that results from being marginalized, unseen, and unheard prepares transgender people to listen to the people they lead and to dedicate their leadership to supporting professional and personal development. Someone who had chosen to transition is someone who had done the work of self-discovery. A transgender leader therefore understands the process of finding one's values and finding oneself on the road to living life as fully as possible.

Fram and Cavallaro explain that transgender leaders have a special social awareness that comes from a lifetime of having to read the room. Queer and trans folks always have to be aware of who in the room might be a threat and who might be an understanding ally. They listen for little clues to cultural competence, like someone asking whether you have a "partner" rather than asking if you have a "husband." This social awareness is a leadership super boost.

Transgender people may have an inherent advantage when it comes to perspective taking. Because of the nature of the accusations that my department had experienced, it occurred to me that men and women might have different perspectives, and I wanted to make sure I understood what everyone was seeing. It occurred to me that I might be in a special position to hear and bridge multiple perspectives.

Fram and Cavallaro point to creativity and innovation among queer and transgender leaders. Such leaders have spent a lifetime engaged in problem-solving. Sometimes the challenge is administrative, like having to find your gender on a form where the possibilities are limited, or just getting a driver's license. A friend of mine who is a trans woman faced the task of selling a vehicle that was registered to her in her former name and gender. Her very practical solution was to rustle through her closet for the most masculine clothing she could find, pull her hair back, and just go down to the motor vehicles office to get the job done. She was, however, delighted when she approached the counter and was asked, "How can I help you, ma'am?"

Often, the challenge that queer and trans folks face is social, demanding the real-time navigation of a conversation that has become suddenly awkward. These small and large problem-solving experiences leave a transgender leader prepared for creative and innovative problem-solving.

Transgender people may have experience with advocacy and activism. It is hard to make it to adulthood as a transgender person without life handing you an opportunity to advocate for yourself. I sued the province of Ontario so I would be recognized as a parent to my children. I've worn a "Silence equals death" T-shirt to protests at City Hall. I show up to Pride events whenever I can. I talk to people when their children come out as transgender. I talk to trans children and support their journeys. A lifetime of activism develops a transgender leader with both practical knowledge of how to navigate the system and the conviction required to do it (Fram & Cavallaro, 2024).

I started to believe my department would benefit from having a transgender leader. Although I was quiet and probably spent less time socializing than my peers did, I did have good relationships with folks in the department. I pictured myself sitting in the chair's office. I contemplated leadership. I imagined being the one who attended to my department's needs. But I was aware that the opportunity was dangerous. As a transman, I was somewhat vulnerable, even though my transition had been well accepted when I returned from a year-long sabbatical with updated pronouns. What if my gender made it easy for people to link my department's tarnished reputation to mine? What if my elevation into a leadership role made me conspicuous enough to attract transphobia? What if becoming chair was career limiting? What if it ruined my career? The decision required some bravery.

I phoned Melanie in New Mexico. She knew about all of the devastation in our department, she knew that we were selecting a new department chair, and she knew that no one had volunteered to take the position. When I told her "I think I need to chair the department," she said, "I know." She couldn't have been less surprised. Of course, she understood that my next five years were going to be intense, but she knew it was the right thing to do. She understood that my department needed me. So, I answered the call.

On May 12, 2021, with 45 minutes left before the deadline, I sent in my application. My email read

> My willingness has a simple motivation: I love my department. I am in awe of my colleagues and their compassion and support for one another. I am touched by their dedication to our students. As always, I admire my colleagues' commitment to excellence in teaching and research, and their sincere desire to help us develop into a better university. I want to do what I can to help build the solid foundation that my department needs in order to do the excellent research and teaching that brings us all together.

I was invited to an interview with the committee that I had so recently left. They asked me, for example, how I "would most effectively engage various stakeholder groups in strategic planning in the Department," and "Please comment on the morale/climate/dynamics in the Department, and how would you influence positive change."

As the only applicant, I got the job.

A Perilous Path

I imagined that I could make a meaningful difference as the first transgender department chair. I would be a visible role model. I would make it apparent that trans people can lead. Transgender leadership in academia is not unprecedented: Aaron Devor is a transman who has served as department chair, dean of graduate studies, and chair in transgender studies at the University of Victoria. Still, trans leadership is exceptionally rare.

Once I had answered the call, I felt confident in my decision to become chair. I had responded to the dean's struggle to fill the position. I believed I could guide the department to values-based leadership. I invested in my leadership development: Over the next few years, I took every leadership course that was available on campus, from a strategic leadership course to a course designed to recognize the mental health needs of employees. I completed an Inclusive Excellence Leadership

Program offered on campus. Off campus, I enrolled in an anti-racism course called "White People Work," and Cornell's Fostering an Inclusive Climate course. I completed the extremely practical and applicable "Leadership Essentials" course. I became proactive about honing my leadership skills and finding opportunities to learn. My approach was to be humble and open to development.

I saw a path, and I was determined. People needed care. People needed to be heard. They needed calm, and they needed the space to connect with their leader and with each other. I told one of my most senior colleagues, "The department is going to be okay."

If I'm honest, I expected undying gratitude from my boss for stepping into an essential role that no one else wanted. What I got was a place on the hot seat.

I got the job but not the gratitude.

The next five years proved to be the most challenging in my life. My reputation, my career, my family, and my health were in jeopardy. Soon I would be asked to resign.

References

Devine, P. G. (1989). Stereotypes and prejudice: Their automatic and controlled components. *Journal of Personality and Social Psychology, 56*(1), 5. https://doi.org/10.1037/0022-3514.56.1.5

Fazio, R. H., Sanbonmatsu, D. M., Powell, M. C., & Kardes, F. R. (1986). On the automatic activation of attitudes. *Journal of Personality and Social Psychology, 50*(2), 229. https://doi.org/10.1037/0022-3514.50.2.229

Fram, B., & Cavallaro, E. (2024). *Forging queer leaders: How the LGBTQIA+ community creates impact from adversity.* Jessica Kingsley Publishers.

Greenwald, A. G., & Banaji, M. R. (1995). Implicit social cognition: Attitudes, self-esteem, and stereotypes. *Psychological Review, 102*(1), 4. https://doi.org/10.1037/0033-295X.102.1.4

Ryan, M. K., & Haslam, S. A. (2005). The glass cliff: Evidence that women are over-represented in precarious leadership positions. *British Journal of Management, 16*(2), 81–90. https://doi.org/10.1111/j.1467-8551.2005.00433.x

2

Transitions: Oregon Farm Kid to Activist and Academic

I was five years old the first time I remember articulating my gender. I told my mom that I wanted to be a boy. If she was shocked, she didn't show it. We were in the upstairs bathroom of our 1892 Victorian farmhouse. She was preparing to paper the walls, and I was perched on top of the ladder, chatting with her. As a young child, I could often be found wherever it was that my hippie homemaker mom was working, whether it was making soap, harvesting honey, or starting a batch of homemade granola. We spent hours talking.

When I was 2, my family moved to a farm in Oregon, five miles from the small town of McMinnville where my father had grown up. He had moved to McMinnville from Iowa when he was seven years old, and his family lived above the small five and dime store that his parents owned and operated. From the age of seven, I worked at "Rutherford's Variety Store" on main street, a store that my grandfather had opened. Our Victorian farmhouse was old and run-down when we moved there, and my parents spent my childhood renovating, painting, and repairing. In the early 1970s, McMinnville was a town of about 14,000 people in what is now Oregon's wine country. Our crops were wheat and Christmas trees.

I had been called a tomboy all my life, mucking around on the family farm and hanging with the group of neighborhood boys every summer, but this was decades before terms like non-binary, transgender, gender independent, or drag king had become part of my vocabulary. We rode bicycles enacting scenes from Starsky and Hutch and pretended to drive the tractors that were parked in the barn. In my preteen years, no one objected to my gender, and I felt pretty comfortable being me.

When I was 5, I had an early experience of what I call gender euphoria—when I feel like my gender is being seen and understood and reflected back to me—and that euphoric feeling clicks into place. My brother and I were performing in a run of "Annie Get Your Gun" at the Gallery Players of Oregon, a local amateur theater.

I was just a kid in the chorus, but my brother played a main character, Annie's younger brother, Little Jake. One day, my brother came down with something and was unable to perform. I told my mom that I could play his part. I had never rehearsed it, but I had attended every rehearsal so I knew all the lines and could mimic my brother's inflections. The director let me play Little Jake that night, and I, for the first time, appeared dressed as a boy, sporting a boy's name. When my mom tucked me into bed that night, I told her, "Today was my proudest day!"

At six years old I was enrolled in kindergarten at Newby Elementary School. Newby is a title A1 school in the lower-income part of McMinnville, Oregon. One spring day, at recess, my friend Ronnie declared that today was "boys-chase-the-girls day." Ronnie was a friendly, well-liked kid who often impressed us by popping wheelies and spinning around in his wheelchair. He had been using a wheelchair ever since his babysitter accidentally shot him in the neck the previous year. Once the chase was declared, there was no way to rein it in. For the entire recess period, a dozen boys chased girls around the black asphalt that demarcated our elementary school playground.

My distinct gender was apparent, at least subconsciously, to my classmates. Not a single boy tried to chase me. Still, the idea that I could be a boy, chasing girls, was beyond the bounds of social expectations back then. I was uncategorical. As boys swarmed and girls scattered, I protected the girls. Girls who were being chased ran to me and hid behind me while the boys who were in pursuit ran off to find easier targets. It was understood by all that this would be my role. No one had to declare that I was occupying a role beyond the binary, not even Ronnie.

In retrospect, I find it remarkable that this happened without discussion. Even the teachers were unsurprised by the role I played that day. Even without the benefit of community or vocabulary, I knew who I was, and I was comfortable being me. Had I been confronted, I would have been unable to explain myself, but no one on the playground on that day in 1973 in rural Oregon required an explanation. This was decades before the current anti-trans moment. In the 1970s, trans people weren't part of the national conversation, and my gender nonconformity flew under the radar.

From my earliest recollection, leadership was a family tradition. During our years on the farm, my father launched a political career. He first ran for the state legislature when I was in kindergarten. Throughout my childhood, election night parties were held in our home, and they were exciting. I had a house full of people who were rooting for the same team and eagerly anticipating the outcome. I thought that election night was one of the biggest holidays of the year.

It was a time of consciousness raising and political action. My parents were both socially liberal feminists. At the time, they were also both republicans. In the 1970s, the republican party of Oregon did not resemble the current national party. Oregon republicans were fiscally responsible and socially laissez-faire with a strong libertarian vibe. As a republican state legislator, my father had supported "gay marriage," three decades before Oregon legalized it. My parents strongly messaged the idea that girls could do anything. They read Ms. Magazine, discussed Gloria Steinem, cheered on Billie Jean King, and were all for "Women's Lib" and the Equal Rights Amendment. My dad wore a T-shirt that said, "A man of quality is not threatened by a woman of equality." When Dianne Feinstein or Chris Evert was in the news, they made sure I knew about it. They introduced me to women who were scientists and when I briefly showed some interest in being a heart surgeon, they introduced me to a friend of theirs who was a heart surgeon.

One of the accomplished women that my parents introduced me to as a child was particularly intriguing to me—a biology teacher named Marian. She took me out to a stream where we scooped up some water, took it back to her classroom, and examined the specimen under a microscope. I was amazed to see tiny protozoa and algae, even though the water appeared clear to the naked eye. I learned decades later that she was a lesbian. In retrospect, that explained the camaraderie I felt with her.

Being Benched and Being Seen

I spent my childhood being generally comfortable being myself. I didn't grow up hating my body or wondering if I was a mistake. I took the whole package, my body, and my gender, for granted, and the whole package seemed coherent to me. My body fit my gender because it was my body, and I was me. Along the way, I had some misunderstandings and some disappointments, but I also had many instances of gender euphoria.

My parents were remarkably willing to engage in deliberate gender transgressions. When I was in second grade, they tried to enroll me in cub scouts, the precursor to the Boy Scouts of America. My enrollment was flatly rejected. We sat through the information meeting in a classroom in my elementary school, just as we had when my brother became a cub scout, but unlike my brother, I did not get to wear the hat, the blue shirt, neckerchief, and enviably cool neckerchief slide. I secretly read the scout book and taught myself the neckerchief fold.

My parents did successfully enroll me in a local wrestling club when I was eight years old. At home, wrestling was a pretty fundamental part of the way I played with my brother and my dad. It made sense to me and to my parents that I might learn some skills and safety. This local club was meant for boys, but that wasn't obvious to me because it was called "Kids' Wrestling." My parents insisted that I be allowed to join for that reason. Was I not a kid? The organizers, who turned out to be small-town volunteers rather than well-organized bigots, relented, but not before I came to understand that I was not wanted. I was so mortified that

I remained on the bench. My parents took me to every practice, but I stayed on the bleachers, red with shame, and that was a fine solution from the organizer's point of view. I couldn't make sense of why I was unwanted.

When I was 10, I got a job picking strawberries at Alderman Farms. The strawberry field was a dynamic mix of cultures. There were lots of kids like me, bringing a slapdash work ethic and making pennies, and there were also adults who did this for a living, picking much more efficiently and ending each day with an impressive haul. Each morning, we were assigned to a row, and over time we got to know the people working nearby. But we didn't introduce ourselves by name; we just chatted off and on all day long. One day I heard one of my fellow strawberry pickers refer to me with male pronouns. I was called "he." I was delighted to hear that I had been perceived as a boy. I didn't correct the kid, and I never did tell him my name.

My family attended the First Unitarian Society of Salem, Oregon. The adults went to services upstairs, and the kids went to the basement for Sunday school. When I was 10 years old, I had a teacher in Sunday school who engaged the kids in some active learning. We went outside when the weather permitted, we studied logic using the game WFF 'N PROOF, and we dissected a pig to increase our understanding of mammalian anatomy. As we got to know each other over many weeks of Sundays, he referred to me with male pronouns. I never asked him to. My mother was perplexed when they would discuss my activities after Sunday school. She tried to correct the pronouns, but he was persistent. I had met someone who understood me years before I was capable of explaining who I was. I really enjoyed spending time with this teacher and hearing my pronouns. I felt gender euphoria. I felt seen.

I also experienced gender-related disappointment, discrimination, and eventually, gender dysphoria. In my experience, gender dysphoria usually happens in a flash. I suddenly see a disconnect between how others see me and how I see myself. It is a deeply uncomfortable feeling. It makes me feel exposed and misunderstood at the same time. It is deflating.

When I was around 10, I really wanted overalls and cowboy boots. Since I lived on a farm in the West, I was pretty sure I needed the outfit. I could picture it very clearly in my head: overalls made of faded denim with metal buckles over rugged leather boots. When the gift arrived, it was nothing like what I had pictured. The overalls were a pristine dark blue, made from a denim thinner than I had ever felt. The buckles were not metal but were bright red and made out of plastic. I had no idea there were overalls like this. These overalls were clearly not made for shoveling manure in the barn. Worse, the cowboy boots had high heels. Crestfallen, I placed the outfit permanently in my closet.

When I was in high school, my dad gave me a book called *The Great Women* by Joan Marlow. The book cover announced, "The inspiring stories of 60 outstanding women of all ages and nations." This was one of his attempts to let me know that I could be anything I wanted to be. Each chapter was a story about a different person: Joan of Arc, Eleanor Roosevelt, Amelia Earhart, Dorothea Dix, George Eliot, Harriet Tubman, Susan B. Anthony, Florence Nightingale, Marie Curie, Helen Keller, and others who had led remarkable lives. I read them all and admired the accomplishments that required each protagonist to overcome sexism to pursue a career. But there was one story that captured my imagination more than all of the others. It was the story of James Barry.

Barry might not have appreciated being included in an anthology about great women. Starting at the age of 15 he lived his life as a man. Born in County Cork in 1789, Barry was assigned female at birth. He moved to London as a teenager and studied to become a tutor, but without any work history, Barry found no such position available to him. Barry took the name of a recently deceased uncle, got a medical degree from the University of Edinburgh, decades before the university was admitting women, and lived and passed as a man for the rest of his life. He joined the British Army and served as a surgeon all over the British Empire.

Maybe I really could be anything I wanted to be.

Propriety and Performance

My father has a definite sense of propriety, and he tried hard to teach me how to be proper. As a politician, he thought the family needed to look appropriate: He expected me to dress like a girl. At times, his expectations were fairly specific. Women should not carry anything in their pockets. Every woman needs a signature cologne. Socially acceptable presentation was especially important during campaigns, when we were all required to look and act as normal as possible. I wore a skirt when I posed with my father on the day he was appointed state treasurer and became one of the highest-ranking republicans in Oregon. I would have preferred a snappy blazer and trousers, but I was proud of my dad and dressed as required.

I went to the same high school my father had attended. He had been elected student body president, and so was I, 30 years later. Throughout my time at McMinnville high school, I had a close friend named Andy. We were in all of the advanced classes together, we were both on student council, and we both had perfect attendance. At the end of our last year in high school, the school held an academic honors assembly, awarding a number of subject-based awards. The most esteemed award was the Academic Excellence Award, which came with a watch and $500. The school always gave the award to one boy and one girl. At the culmination of the assembly, Andy and I were called down to the front of the gymnasium that served as the venue for the ceremony. The award was announced to great applause, and we smiled proudly. We were each handed our prizes.

He opened his box, revealing a golden watch with a huge round face and a bold leather strap. I opened my box and found.... a much smaller watch. The face was about half the diameter of his. The strap was dainty. We had received the same award, but I had been given a delicate piece of jewelry. I wasn't just disappointed, I was embarrassed. I felt misunderstood.

Getting Closer

I left McMinnville in 1987, and I attended Yale University. My plan was to get a BA then attend graduate school and eventually become a professor. I had thought about becoming a lawyer like my father, but a PhD was more appealing because being called "Dr. Rutherford" would get me out of being referred to with a gendered title for the rest of my life.

It was rare to be out in the late 1980s and at Yale I was very out, as a lesbian. I was so out that my classmate Jodi Rudoren phoned me for comment any time there was any gay-related news on campus. The women on the floor in my residence were not happy about me living among them. One time, when I tried to have a conversation with a roommate about homophobia, she proudly declared, "I'm not a homophobe, I'm a homo hater!" I felt so unsafe in my dorm that I eventually called my dad and asked him to get me out of there. He took me to Kentucky for the weekend. It was a different world, a time of overt and unapologetic discrimination. Ellen DeGeneres hadn't come out yet.

Before I went to graduate school at the University of California, Santa Barbara, I took a couple of years off to live in San Francisco. When I was a kid, we had a college student named Mark move into our house for a few months to do some caretaking and some babysitting. He was gay, and when he left our house, he moved to San Francisco, so I knew that that was where my people lived.

I moved there in 1992, the year the San Francisco pride committee dubbed, "The year of the queer." I was living through my first pandemic, and at the time, it was believed that becoming infected with HIV was a death sentence. With very few exceptions, it was. The queer community had been alarmed into activism. People wore "Silence = Death" T-shirts and yelled "Act Up! Fight Back!" in the streets. Every walk down Market Street was dotted with billboards telling me to "Be here for the cure." The pain was current, and the fear was palpable. The visibility and political power that resulted from communal defiance was new.

When I lived there, I rode a motorcycle and wore leather chaps and a leather motorcycle jacket. My friends were all queer, including Theo whose transition from female to male, is described in a documentary called "A Boy named Sue," directed and edited by my friend Julie Wyman. Theo introduced me to other trans guys and broadened my understanding of life as a transman. The film followed

Theo's transition over six years, so among other lessons, I learned that transition is a process that takes longer than a day of surgery.

In those years, in that city, in those clothes, I was experiencing gender euphoria. I thought that my gender presentation was clear, and I was confident that everyone could see who I was. Although I traveled almost exclusively in queer circles, there were times when I had to emerge from the Castro district to interact with straight, cisgender people. I came face to face with a cisgender man when I took a driving test to get my motorcycle license.

When you take a motorcycle test, you have to stay in view of the examiner while they stand in the parking lot, so that they can observe you throughout your ride. My examiner told me to turn left, then turn right, and then stop quickly. I had to drive in a full circle and then in an even smaller circle. This was easy enough for me and I was pretty sure I had passed. He called me over and asked me to park the bike, dismount, and stand in front of him. Then he asked me to remove my helmet. That didn't seem strange to me until he said, "Thanks, I just wanted to see your pretty eyes."

I was wearing leather from shoulder to toe and presenting as a butch dyke. In San Francisco, I knew a few women who were more butch than I was, but I was pretty butch. I am not sure what the examiner's intention was. Did he want to diminish me? To challenge me? To cast femininity upon me? I felt exposed and misunderstood at the same time.

The same year, I also experienced gender euphoria. I traveled to Thailand to spend a couple of weeks with Eva, a friend of mine from Yale. I flew into Bangkok and stayed with her in the tiniest apartment I've ever seen. She was teaching English as a second language to women who worked in the sex industry and had English-speaking clients. These women wanted to learn English so that they would be able to negotiate their boundaries and their fees. I went with her to the language school during the day and later to the bar where her students started their evenings. After our days in Bangkok, we traveled up to Chiang Mai to visit markets and temples. When our rented motorcycle popped a tire, we had to decide who should drive to get it fixed, Eva, who spoke Thai, or me, with my motorcycle license. I went off to get the tire fixed. It turns out not much language is necessary when you can point to your flat tire.

A more subtle, more relevant, aspect of language usage emerged during our travels. In the Thai language, there is a syllable that is added to the end of every sentence to make it polite and respectful. That syllable depends on your gender. Men add "kháp" to the end of their utterances. The women and the drag queens that we were spending time with used "khá." As we traveled around, I noticed people walking out of shops and homes to say hello to me, either "Sawatdee kháp" or "Sawatdee khá." I asked Eva if people were always this friendly in rural Thailand. She said that they were talking to me hoping that I would say something back. They found my gender ambiguous, and if I said anything to them, I would have to say kháp or khá. Once I understood what they needed, I smiled and replied "Sawatdee kháp!" It was comforting to have such an easy way of being seen as me.

In graduate school, while I was earning a PhD in psychology, I took a course in child language development. An assignment required me to go to a playground at the UC Santa Barbara day care and record the kids' conversations. We were supposed to be inconspicuous—this wasn't an interview. As I eavesdropped near a group of four-year-olds, they began to talk about me. Eventually, a delegate was sent to ask me, "Are you a boy or a girl?" I asked her what she thought. She told me, "You look like a boy, but you sound like a girl," as she returned to her group for further consultation. Eventually, she announced the verdict to her group: "She's a boy!" I smiled at her apt summary.

Namewrecked

I've heard various descriptions and metaphors that trans folks have offered to explain gender dysphoria. The Honorable Sarah McBride, the first transgender member of the US House of Representatives, likens it to homesickness. She found this analogy useful when explaining her gender to her parents. For me, gender dysphoria is what it feels like when someone has learned my sex assigned at birth and thinks that they now understand who I am.

I was named after my great grandmother. It is the kind of name parents give to babies who are assigned female at birth and definitely not the kind of name parents give to boys. I'm not going to tell you the name that I was assigned at birth. I don't use it anymore. In the trans community that expired name is often referred to as a "dead name," and for some people, its use evokes gender dysphoria.

Oddly, my name was never a source of gender dysphoria in my childhood because I never thought of it as a girl's name. I only thought of it as my name. It didn't strike me as feminine because I didn't strike me as feminine. It wasn't a common name, so I didn't often have the opportunity to use this particular name to sort people by gender.

In the end, it was my name that caused me so much gender dysphoria that I realized I had to transition. It was the subject line of a 1999 email virus that spread through Word documents, hijacked over a million accounts, and caused $80 million in damage. The virus disguised itself as a message from a trusted associate, making it feel personal. Something that seemed harmless and familiar turned out to be deeply disruptive.

Nothing about that computer virus and its damage has anything to do with me, except that the virus was named after a stripper who happened to share my given name. This virus was prominent in the news for weeks, and stories always included some mention of the hacker being obsessed with a stripper who bore the name we had in common. My name had never caused me gender dysphoria, but this story, this virus, the sexualization and obsession with this stripper who was so obviously female gave me that feeling. It was the first time it clicked for me that I'd been going around all my life using a girl's name and that people were perceiving me as a girl. I felt exposed and misunderstood. I needed to make a change, and I did. Since that time, I've been called Mel.

Love and Marriage

After I completed my doctorate, I moved to Colorado for a postdoctoral fellowship at the University of Denver. While in Colorado, I met my future wife, Melanie, at the Jefferson Unitarian Church in Golden, Colorado. She had joined the church and had started a young adults group because she wanted to meet a man. She met me.

We got to know each other over several months while planning and attending events with this group. It wasn't love at first sight, but we were both committed to the young adults group she was building, so we kept finding opportunities to talk. Sometimes we were the only two who showed up for events, and over time, we got to know each other.

After a few months, we realized there was an attraction, which for her forced a reckoning. Why was she attracted to me if she wasn't queer? I loaned her Leslie Feinberg's book *Stone Butch Blues*, which the author describes as "a lesbian novel and a transgender novel." The novel follows the life of Jess, a fictionalized version of the author, who interacts with the world as a woman, as a man, and as a genderqueer person, navigating love, sex, and employment. Melanie and I talked about my gender. We began dating.

While in Colorado, I also joined a transgender support group. There was a men's support group that I attended monthly, and it felt like a homecoming because I had never hung out with so many trans guys before. One was a firefighter and another was a minister. One was a single parent and others were in long-term relationships. One guy was single and really wanted to be dating a man but lamented that he couldn't find one who was interested in dating a trans guy.

Sometimes the men's group and the women's group met together, and from time to time, the group opened up to "SOFFAs," significant others, friends, family, and allies. Melanie attended a meeting as a SOFFA. She was developing her understanding of her identity and mine. Then I was offered a faculty position in Canada, a country that Melanie had never visited before.

Fatherhood in Two Countries

Two years later, when I was 36 years old, Melanie and I had twins. I had always known that I wanted children, but queer couples have some logistical hurdles when it comes to making babies. Emerson and Xander were conceived by harvesting my eggs which were fertilized using donor sperm and implanted in Melanie. We were happy that we were both undeniably their parents, at least until our parenthood was denied.

Parenthood is exhilarating and exhausting. I was in the room when our twins were born. I got to cut Xander's umbilical cord, and I got to carry Emerson from the delivery room to the NICU. With no formal training, we brought tiny twins home from the hospital and had the responsibility of taking care of their every need. With two of them, they could keep us busy day and night. The love was abundant, and we nurtured our little people. They grew, developed, and eventually smiled. I was tired, and I was happy.

Melanie and I learned that our family had gotten ahead of the law. Although the province had approved our marriage, it was not ready to recognize both of us as parents. There was simply no legal mechanism. Under the law at the time, one of us would have had to adopt our children, which didn't make sense to us. We sued the province of Ontario and won the right to put both of our names on our children's birth certificates. We had started the legal action before they were born, so our kids, both under five pounds at birth, came into this world as tiny social justice advocates. They were plaintiffs at birth.

Our case was part of a class action lawsuit involving four couples, but we were the only ones who had used IVF with an anonymous sperm donor in a way that gave us both a clear biological connection to our children. Because of this, the province settled its case with us, recognizing us both as legal parents, even before the other couples' cases were heard in court. Our decision then set a legal precedent for the other three families even though they each had their own path to parenthood. They went on to win the case as well. The case, *Rutherford v. Ontario*, became a precedent in the province. Now, any couple in Ontario who uses anonymous donor sperm to make their family can list both parents on their child's birth certificate.

Once the problem was solved in Ontario, we had to deal with the United States. We filed an application for passports for our kids at the US consulate in Toronto, but they could not be processed until our children had their Consular Report of Birth Abroad documents, a document that is like a birth certificate, but for US citizens who were born outside the country. We didn't want that document issued without both of our names on it as parents. Although Melanie and I were married in Ontario and we were both listed on the kids' birth certificates, the US Federal government would have issued these documents listing me as a single unwed mother. They wouldn't recognize our marriage, they wouldn't recognize my gender, and they wouldn't recognize Melanie as a parent.

When our children were born, George W. Bush was president. We decided the best strategy for navigating the U.S. federal government was just to wait it out until the administration changed. Our opportunity came when Barack Obama became president in 2009. Our case was sent to Hillary Clinton as the Secretary of State. She saw that we were married, she saw that we were both the biological parents of our twins, and it made sense that both of our names should be on their documents. With a new federal administration in place, the documents for our children came easily and did not require a court battle. You know the phrase "choose your battles," but we learned that sometimes delaying the battle, waiting for a friendlier administration, is an effective approach to activism.

The next question was what were the kids going to call me? I would have been happy with the kids referring to me as "Daddy," but this was three years before I transitioned and it would have been awkward, even potentially unsafe, for them to do so. Instead, they called me "Teddy." The name was borrowed from Melanie's daughter who had called me "Teddy," short for "Teddy Bear," when she first met me. When I transitioned, they started calling me "Dad" all on their own.

When we enrolled them in preschool, I still had not transitioned but I thought it was clear to everyone that I was their dad. In retrospect this may have been clearer in my mind than it was to others. In any case, when Mother's Day came along, and the kids set about making their crafty present for their mom (an empty orange-juice concentrate container elaborately decorated and intended for use as a pencil holder), I explained to the teachers that the kids would make their Mother's Day craft for Melanie, and their Father's Day craft for me. They looked relieved. This seemed to be the answer to a question that they didn't know how to ask.

Taking My Shot

I may have known for years that I was not like everyone else, but it wasn't until I approached my 40th birthday that I felt it was time to transition. My family was complete. I had earned tenure at my university, so I assumed that my job would not be in jeopardy. My niece and nephew were getting older, and I didn't want to be anyone's "aunt." An upcoming sabbatical provided the perfect opportunity to transition. There was no reason to wait.

Even after I had decided that I was ready, it was a bit of a struggle to get permission to transition. I told my family doctor, who was supportive but since she had never managed a gender affirming transition before, she referred me to Toronto's

Centre for Addiction and Mental Health (CAMH). At the time, CAMH was using the Harry Benjamin's Standards of Care for gender affirming transition which meant that they would not aid in my transition until I could document that I had lived a year of "Real-Life Experience" as a man. I would need a note from my employer saying that I was living as a man at work. That requirement struck me as not just awkward, but dangerous. I was just supposed to pass as a man, without the aid of testosterone? I knew someone who had been beaten nearly to death for that kind of gender ambiguity. I left CAMH and went back to my family doctor who gave me a prescription for testosterone.

I started taking testosterone in April of 2008. Within a couple of months of taking testosterone, people who had never met me before perceived me as a man. My mood evened out. I felt more stable, and I had the feeling that everything was going to be okay. And I felt hot. Sometimes when I worked out at the gym it was hours before I stopped sweating, even after a shower. Melanie and I could finally participate in the battle over the thermostat that heterosexual couples had previously monopolized.

When I told my dad, then 71, that I was taking testosterone and transitioning to live as a man, he seemed relieved. He told me that he was taking testosterone too, and we bonded over our common experience of the effects of testosterone, including the fact that it makes it harder to cry. He is still very conscious of propriety, including gender norms. Now instead of telling me how to sit, he instructs me to wait until all of the women have exited the elevator before I do so.

On July 1st of 2008, I started a year-long sabbatical in Albuquerque, New Mexico. The plan was to look more masculine when I returned and also to tell everyone at some point during the year that my pronouns were he and him. That was a good plan for people I wouldn't be seeing for a year, but what about Melanie and the rest of our family? I had to actually give them a date. There had to be a moment when everyone started using the new pronouns. The hard work in the pronoun update was theirs, not mine since I almost always use first-person pronouns to refer to myself.

We had just arrived in Albuquerque and started attending the First Unitarian Church of Albuquerque. No one there knew us, and no one knew my gender history. I had been on testosterone for 4 months when we went on a camping trip with about 25 members of our new church. This was a period of perceptual ambiguity for me: people who already knew me didn't really perceive any change, certainly not a categorical change, while people who had never met me might not be sure which of two genders I fit into. This camping trip was the weekend before my pronoun update, and it didn't make much sense to meet a bunch of new friends using pronouns that would be obsolete in a week. So, we didn't use any gendered pronouns during the long weekend, and—this was back in 2008—nobody asked.

My mom came for a visit, and we all decided that on September 1, they would begin using "he" and "him" when referring to me. They would practice together and reinforce each other. They were quite good at it, but as you may know if you've been through this, there are slips, especially when telling stories of the past.

During my year-long sabbatical, when testosterone was changing my face, my voice, and my body, I needed to tell people who weren't with me about my pronouns. I didn't want to tell some people and make them keep it a secret. Instead, I wanted everyone in each of my communities to know at the same time. So, I had three big coming out moments: to my church, to my extended family, and to my colleagues in my department at work. Church was first and easiest. I was confident that in my church, everyone was going to get my pronouns right or wither in embarrassment. Two people in my church had started using male pronouns with me before I ever asked them to. My extended family was fine when I sent all of my aunts and cousins an email telling them that I was taking testosterone and would be using male pronouns. I got some supportive replies, including from cousins I hadn't seen in years.

In my department at work, my strategy was to tell the students working in my lab as a group, then tell my boss, and then send an email to each of my colleagues. My closest personal relationship was with my students, and I didn't want them to hear about my transition from someone else first. When I took a trip to Canada and sat down with my students in my lab, I had been taking testosterone for about six months, so my voice was already sounding deeper. I told them that when I got back from sabbatical, I would be using the pronouns he and him, and I invited them to practice my pronouns while I was away in Albuquerque. They seemed to take it in stride. I told my boss, the chair of my department, that I would be using new pronouns when I returned. She said she would do her best to use my new pronouns, but mostly just stopped using pronouns when talking about me. Then I sent an email to each of my colleagues:

> I'm writing my friends and colleagues in order to let everyone know that when I am back in the department on July 1st, I will be asking people to use masculine pronouns when referring to me. My appearance has already changed somewhat and will continue to change so that eventually this will seem natural. I wanted to keep you in the loop now, because I realize that people are starting to have conversations with potential honours thesis and graduate students and it will be less awkward for anyone joining my lab next year if people are consistent. I have talked to everyone in my own lab, and I have talked with our chair. Please don't feel worried about slip-ups and fumbles ... it will take some time to get used to. This will seem difficult and artificial for a while, and then eventually it won't.
>
> I'm having a great time in Albuquerque, and hope all is well back home.
>
> Soon,
> Mel

I have been so fortunate to work with these people. Nobody seemed shocked. Some people emailed me back with congratulations. One person said that they had been through a pronoun update with friends before. Another said they would prefer that we all use "they," but would follow my lead. Most responses included updates about what people were up to back home, with a brief acknowledgment of my "heads-up" email and their commitment to try the new pronouns. All of them made me feel welcome and included in the department.

Eventually, I had to come out to my own kids. They were born before I transitioned, but I don't think they ever perceived me as anything but dad. A few years after our sabbatical in Albuquerque, Melanie called me at work and said she was coming to pick me up. The kids had started to ask questions! She didn't feel equipped to decide what to reveal and what was private. Emerson and Xander were fascinated. Wide-eyed, they asked, "You mean you have been in a girl's bathroom?" as if that somehow made me a rockstar. They wanted to know whether my ears were pierced. They are.

Their experience with having a trans dad has been mostly neutral, sometimes positive, and occasionally negative. They have attended Pride annually, have a very competent and contemporary vocabulary, and are very good at updating pronouns. Having access to the queer and trans community has enriched their lives.

However, we once had a family with three kids over for an afternoon of snacks and games, and after we came out to them, we never saw them again. We liked them, and it was jarring. After that experience, Emerson was very careful when making a new friend. He always asks, "Do his parents know?" He is not going to invest in a friendship that might vanish.

Transitioning to Leadership

I had transitioned at work over 13 years before I became chair, and my colleagues were more than accepting—they made it easy. But would my transition be a barrier to my stepping into a leadership role?

In a survey of 132 corporate leaders, Out & Equal (2023) found that 14% of transgender leaders reported that their relationships at work were worse after they came out. Forty-three percent of transgender leaders reported experiencing discrimination due to their gender identity, and 71% reported that their gender identity was the primary source of bias that they experienced in the workplace.

Given how rare transgender and non-binary leadership is at the highest levels of academia, politics, and the corporate world, it is uncommon for transgender leaders to find mentorship from people who share their gender identity. I had never reported to a transgender leader, and I knew of no trans people at my university who were in leadership. In fact, years earlier when I approached the DEI office to suggest that there might be a networking event for transgender faculty members, I was told that I was the only one on campus.

A myriad of personality and demographic traits can impact whether an individual is seen as a strong, capable leader, and this can be mediated by gender. Strategies and approaches to leadership can be perceived differently depending on the gender of the leader (Andrade, 2023), and if a leader's strategy is inconsistent with stereotypes, this mismatch can actually impact whether the leader is successful (Bowen et al., 2000). If women are expected to be quiet, a commanding approach to leadership may be viewed negatively. To date very little research has looked at whether transgender and gender non-binary identities impact leadership effectiveness or perceived effectiveness.

I grew up in a household where leadership was modeled. Early in my life, I had experiences as a student leader, but that was years before I transitioned. When I became department chair in 2021, I had to deal with a number of anti-trans stereotypes and an escalating anti-trans backlash. Little did I know that my superiors' disdain for me would become so forceful I would question whether I was welcome at my university. I was facing the worst crisis of my career.

References

Andrade, M. S. (2023). Personality and leadership: How gender impacts perceptions of effectiveness. *Strategic HR Review, 22*(1), 2–6. https://doi.org/10.1108/SHR-09-2022-0052

Bowen, C. C., Swim, J. K., & Jacobs, R. R. (2000). Evaluating gender biases on actual job performance of real people: A meta-analysis. *Journal of Applied Social Psychology, 30*(10), 2194–2215. https://doi.org/10.1111/j.1559-1816.2000.tb02432.x

Out & Equal (2023). Experiences of The Lavender Ceiling: Progress and continued challenges facing out LGBTQ+ leaders at work. Out & Equal Workplace Advocates. https://www.winus.org/includion-and-belonging-library/experiences-of-the-lavender-ceiling-progress-and-continued-challenges-facing-lgbtq-leaders-at-work/

3

Communication and Chaos in the Information Desert

On June 24, 2021, after the investigations into the allegations were complete, the president of the university announced that accused staff, faculty, and a student would be reintegrated into my department. The president said legal limitations did not allow him to share the specific responses to individual issues but "… the process found allegations were not substantiated and policies were not violated. Where appropriate, interim measures have been removed and individuals are being reintegrated into the University community." He hoped that "awareness of the outcomes, and knowing that formal threat assessments have been conducted, will provide assurance of the university's commitment to safety." He trusted the update would provide "some clarity and begin to bring some closure."

One week later, I was the chair of the department, and it was my job to do the reintegration.

Hundreds of people were now in my care. I was determined to do a good job. For some people, my task was just to reassure them that if we involved ourselves in university governance, we could endeavor to create a safe campus. But with some people, I felt like their lives were in my hands: During the eight months when we were not allowed to communicate with the accused, I wondered about the risk of suicide. It became my job to talk to these people about their future. I felt the weight of this responsibility of care. It felt monumental and daunting, but I was optimistic. I was focused by my commitment to my department.

The reintegration was a challenge. One graduate student refused a teaching assistant assignment with one of the professors who had been accused, even though the student had willingly worked with this professor prior to her being accused. Several faculty members who worked in another department asked me to remove one of the accused from a committee they served on, suggesting that an aversion had developed as a result of the accusations. The shunned faculty member eventually stepped off the committee voluntarily. A faculty member in another department told a university administrator that she was "shocked" that I was supporting the reintegration of people who had been accused of violations of the sexual violence policy. Never mind that it was my job.

Reintegrating people into the community following ruinous publicity would have been a dangerous task for any leader. Anyone who stepped into the role of chair was destined to become the department's spokesperson and public advocate. I imagine that this contributed to the fact that none of my colleagues wanted the job. As a now public transgender figure, I was exposed. The internet is a wild and unmoderated jungle, and women and gender minorities are particularly vulnerable to being attacked online (Jane, 2014). The internet can be an unrelentingly vicious place for transgender people who attract public attention (Nagata et al., 2025). By leaving me the task of clarifying what had happened, the university administration was handing me to the wolves.

As the allegations were being announced throughout 2020, our dean had referred to the number of allegations as "unprecedented," and it was. The university had no experience with a reintegration of this magnitude. As allegations were announced, the cleanup was never contemplated. No one from the administration reached out to me to discuss how I would reintegrate people who had been accused, people with a now tarnished reputation, into my department. They were not sharing their reintegration plan because they had no plan to share with me. It was clear to me that the administration had not contemplated how one could succeed at such a task.

As one concrete example, when I became chair, the door locks to the offices of the accused had been plugged by security services so that no one—not me, not the custodial staff, not the denizens of those offices—could get in. Weeks after people had been cleared of allegations and their reintegration had been publicly announced, the very practical task of unplugging their office locks had been overlooked. I hadn't anticipated that as a new department chair, I would have to figure out that particular puzzle. I was a new leader in a perilous situation facing a complex task. I had no road map.

On June 25, 2021, a week before I took office, my predecessor and I met (via Zoom, of course) with the president and the provost. Our aim was to impress upon them how much the department had been damaged and to ask for their help in repairing the department and its reputation. They had other aims. We heard no sympathy, no offer of help, and a follow-up letter from the president said, "The Provost and I were disappointed that in our meeting you failed to recognize or acknowledge any cultural issues within the PNB Department." Ouch. It was never clear what we were invited to acknowledge because they hadn't shared any details with us about what the "cultural issues" were. They did tell us that "The Provost and I share and support your goal of rebuilding the reputation of the Department, but this can only be achieved through the implementation of concrete initiatives intended to effect positive change." They didn't suggest any concrete initiatives.

Three weeks into my term as chair, the president of the university invited me to what I thought was going to be a one-on-one meeting. You probably understand that "invited" is an understatement. I was summoned, and I was intimidated. By attending this meeting, I wasn't just skipping a level to my boss's boss, I was talking to the boss of my boss's boss. I was skipping both the dean and the provost. He brought his chief of staff, a lawyer. I was naïve and trusting. I thought we were on the same team, so it did not occur to me to bring a lawyer.

It was July 14, 2021, and meetings were still being held remotely. Ontario's lockdown had recently been lifted, and people were traveling internationally again, albeit with face masks and proof of a negative COVID test. My time of isolation at home was over, and I had taken my kids to Oregon to see my mother for the first time in a year and a half. I was in my mom's apartment when I took the Zoom meeting. I was nervous, but I was hopeful that he might be able to shed some light on what had happened and what I could do to be helpful as chair of my department. Sadly, no.

It quickly became clear that the president had not quite appreciated how little communication there had been. I (and others in my department) were in the dark about how these months-long suspensions and tremendous interruptions of our academic mission could have come about. He seemed unaware that while he may have access to all of the reports, no one had shared them with me. He said to me, "As you take over, the first part of this is going to be about looking at all of the information that's been put in front of you and making decisions about what is the best way to move that department forward."

All of the information? Put in front of me?

He appeared sincere in his belief that information had been put in front of me. He really didn't understand how perplexed I was. Why had a handful of members of our department simultaneously been charged with allegations and then returned to work after investigations were complete? Why was our department under scrutiny? I was focused on staying calm and professional, so I didn't shout, "What information!?!" Instead, I said, "In terms of the information, are you planning on sharing any of the reports with me?"

The president consulted his legal advisor, "will the final reports be shared, or…?" His chief of staff said, "Individual investigation reports no, won't be shared." I asked, "What about the report from the systemic review?" The president had ordered an investigation into our department's culture, which he referred to as a systemic review. "That will or will not be shared with me?" "Will not," was his reply. Trying to figure out my next steps, I queried the president more than once about what he thought I, as department chair, could do to move the department forward. The president told me, "I think you set the tone in the department." This seemed a departure from his previous request: "the implementation of concrete initiatives."

Information Desert

I was embarking on the leadership challenge of a lifetime, reintegrating community members who had had serious allegations leveled against them and trying to repair a department in crisis. I needed information and I needed mentorship, but I could not find either of these from our administrators. In fact, they seemed determined to hold the department accountable for.... something.

Meetings that I had with other administrators were no more enlightening than my early meeting with the university president. Within weeks of my becoming chair, the dean told me that there would be no apology, public or private, from the upper administration for the events that had disrupted the academic activities of the department. As time went on, we did not see any remorse or sympathy from our leaders. The just-world fallacy is the psychological tendency to believe that people get what they deserve, and the world is inherently just or fair. People tend to have the intuition that good things happen to good people and bad things happen to people who deserve it (Lerner & Simmons, 1966). Consistent with the just-world hypothesis, the upper administration acted as if these personal and academic disruptions would not have happened to people if they didn't deserve them.

One high-ranking university official invited me into her office where she had laid her table with stacks of paper. She told me that these stacks of paper were her "evidence" that my department had a problematic culture. It almost felt like she was blaming me for a culture that was developed before I was in leadership. It struck me as odd that she referred to this information as "evidence," instead of acting collaboratively to help me develop my departmental culture. If she had information that could help me lead my department, why wouldn't she share it? Was the stack of paper a prop set up to convince me that there was a problem in my department, while providing me with no actionable information? I needed information that would help me lead the department. She told me that our department needs "to be situated in a new culture, not in the past," but she never clarified what the target culture was, nor did she share the supposed secrets these stacks of paper held.

The administration clearly wanted me to make major changes in the "culture" in the department, but I didn't know what their concerns were. If concerns were identified in the "systemic review," wouldn't the department chair be the person who needed to hear those concerns? And if they weren't going to share those concerns with the department chair, the person who could directly influence the culture, then why did they pay more than $600,000 for such a review? What was the point of all of this?

Other communications from our superiors were also confusing and contradictory. Unrelated to the accusation and sanctions, I was sent a brochure encouraging me to build a family-like atmosphere. The brochure described a case study, in which students said their academic program was "comfortable," "supportive," "cohesive," and "energetic" (Posselt et al., 2017, p. 21). The brochure described faculty going beyond their roles in order to support students personally and professionally. Students in the case study described faculty as "warm and approachable," saying this appealed to women and BIPOC students, and led to better student well-being, overall. They concluded by saying that a "family-like" atmosphere was superior to the typical "do your work and leave approach" (Posselt et al., 2017, p. 29).

My colleagues and our current and former students had spent decades intentionally developing a culture that we thought was supportive and reduced barriers to mentorship. I had faculty colleagues who would spend hours chatting with their students about topics ranging from science to professional development. Prior to the systemic review, when a graduate student defended their dissertation, their supervisor would invite the entire department to their home for a celebration, which always included the supervisor extolling the student's triumph. We had built the kind of culture described by Posselt et al. (2017) as a strategy to build a family-like atmosphere. However, in my meeting with the president, I was told, "I recognize some people regard the department as a family culture and a supportive one. I actually don't like that term. I think it's the wrong way to frame the relationship between the faculty and students within that department." I left that meeting feeling like I was not allowed to say our department was like a family. Contradictory messages from the people in charge did neither help me identify "concrete initiatives" nor find a direction for my leadership. I was left with the impression that there were no right answers, only wrong answers.

There was massive confusion among our students and in the department generally about what had caused the crisis and what we should be doing to make people feel safer at work. Were faculty members allowed to talk to students? Were social gatherings allowed? Were we going to continue to gather socially and to celebrate achievements and milestones? The lack of any explanation for the allegations and resulting restrictions that together led to a massive upheaval was a real threat to our department's cohesion. When faced with the unexplained, people will assuage their confusion by creating plausible stories. Different people will generate different stories, each of which is consistent with the available information, but many of which will turn out to be false. The irresistible human tendency to generate plausible hypotheses to explain confusing events has been called confabulation (Roser & Gazzaniga, 2006). The more fear-inducing the situation, the greater the urge to create a plausible explanation, until it becomes irresistible (Adolphs, 2013).

Once multiple stories are generated, a community is extremely vulnerable to breaking into factions. Factions who hold incompatible beliefs can come to see each other as lacking rationality or even lacking morality (De Ridder, 2021). A community in crisis is vulnerable when they are exposed only to low-quality information or no information at all. To their credit, my department never fell into this trap, but when I became chair, the threat was real. The need for high-quality communication was urgent. Brené Brown has told us what we probably already knew: Clear is kind. Unclear is unkind (Brown, 2018).

I was feeling the stress of carrying a massive leadership challenge with no support from my superiors. They didn't have a plan for reintegrating the accused and rebuilding the department, since the university had never worked through this specific leadership challenge before. Still, they were my leaders. Maybe they could help me brainstorm? Maybe something in their experience would suggest a fruitful path to try? Maybe some insight they had from the many reports they had would be helpful? The university's administration was ready to let me embark on the task of repairing the department without giving me any insight into what they thought had led to the series of unsubstantiated allegations. I was left to make inferences based on what I had read in the news. It apparently never occurred to them that I needed information in order to do my job. They were willing to leave me on my own on the Glass Cliff.

One source of support and perspective that I leaned on was other department chairs. In my first year as chair, I initiated a tradition of organizing dinners for all of the chairs in the faculty of science. There were eight of us. I shared some of my challenges and experiences, and we also discussed more mundane administrative and programmatic puzzles that we all faced. One experienced chair met with me to hear my challenges, and since we were still being cautious about meeting indoors, our meeting was a hike through the series of trails through a forest near campus. Another department chair was assigned to be my mentor. I told her about the impact of the disruption on our department. Her reflections on my department's experiences gave me perspective.

I networked with a nationwide group of psychology department chairs. I kept them apprised of what was going on in my department, and they offered support and mentorship. One of them reached out to me for a one-on-one meeting to encourage me. She thought I was showing strong leadership.

I had to think about how to start to bridge my department's communication gap. The first step in moving the department forward was going to be communication. It was up to me to design and implement the transparent communication my department needed.

Deep Listening

During my one-on-one meeting with the university's president, he gave me permission to communicate with our students. Mostly he didn't have any concrete suggestions, but one message that was very clear, even emphatic, was that I could speak to students. When COVID-19 forced us to learn new ways of working and socializing, our associate department chair of graduate students regularly hosted what she called "townhall" meetings, held online, to share information about our COVID procedures and new resources. The town halls provided a human connection for people who were in isolation at home. As allegations were accelerating, she was told by a member of the university's administration that these town hall meetings had to stop. Town hall meetings with students were forbidden or monitored while the allegations were being announced, and my predecessor was told to cancel a meeting with our graduate DEI group. Because of these prohibitions, many of us faculty members were unsure about when and how normal communication with graduate students could resume. Relationships between students and faculty were chilled.

I told the president, "My values and goals are around communication. We've been stymied with all these prohibitions about who we can talk to and how we can talk to our graduate students." I asked, "Is it okay with you if I reach out to the graduate DEI group and speak to them?"

The president replied, "Absolutely. I think you should speak to the students in the department, undergraduate and graduate." He told me, "We're at a point where we want to have open conversation. I think it's completely appropriate, now that you're coming in as a chair, that you initiate those kinds of conversations with all various members of the department."

That was helpful. With his permission, I was ready to listen and learn, but listening gets more difficult as you move into higher positions in the hierarchy. The more power you have within an organization, the more listening can feel like work. It becomes less intuitive (Rutherford, 2004). In addition, when you hold some power over people, you become intimidating, so it becomes harder for the people to open up to you. You have to make people feel safe. You have to create processes that allow you to get insight into what others are thinking. It can be helpful to create multiple channels of communication in order to hear from a variety of people. I was going to have to get to work in order to hear the perspectives in my department. Listening became the focus of my job.

One thing I have learned is that leaders might try to control the flow of information. I was told to communicate by some administrators while others tried to keep me from communicating. This was bewildering, and I am sure it led to some people being frustrated with me when there was no way to satisfy all of the administrators at the same time. I decided to open up communication, as recommended by the President.

In the service of the unhurried, reflective listening our department needed, I started opening more channels of communication. I contacted some students who were members of our student's DEI group. I wanted to hear their perspective. I had several meetings with students who had written an open letter to the president asking for more information so they could make "informed decisions about how to keep ... safe in the workplace." I asked them what they needed. While many people were still working remotely, I moved into the chair's office where I worked with my door open. I went to find and to sit with some of the people who had been most impacted. I offered compassion. I gave people space and time. I listened.

I started holding office hours during which I was available both in person and online, where people could queue up in a Zoom waiting room. The Zoom format offered some anonymity because people didn't have to line up conspicuously in the hallway in front of the chair's office. I was hoping that, by offering office hours, I would hear from students, and I did. Dozens reached out to me, wanting to understand what had happened and what was changing. Were they allowed to have social gatherings? Could faculty and students attend the same social events? Had the university changed its alcohol policy?

There was confusion about the use of alcohol because our dean had appeared on the local news stating that "inappropriate behavior" could be explained by the use of alcohol before the investigations had determined whether there was "inappropriate behavior" to be explained. I was able to clarify that the university's alcohol policy had not changed. The upper administration still holds events where alcohol is served for free, and the university still holds four liquor licenses. Students were still free to imbibe, as long as they were of age and complying with the university's alcohol policy.

Because I was hearing these questions, I circulated the university's alcohol policy to the department. I also circulated a policy that directs a supervisor and student who are in an intimate relationship to immediately create a different supervisory structure. I created a workshop for students that provides strategies for navigating the hierarchy that is academia, and I delivered the workshop to all of our undergraduate students. Transparency seemed to be my best option given that I was supposed to come up with a novel solution without any information about our target condition or even any information about the problem I was trying to solve.

The administration may have painted themselves into a corner when they ordered the systemic review. If we had a sex ring, they needed to determine what it was about our culture that had allowed such a thing. They suspected that alcohol might have had a cause in creating the sex ring in our department and publicly stated that alcohol played a factor in the "inappropriate behavior." When the individual investigations uncovered no sex ring, the picture of a broken department that they had created to explain the sex ring served no purpose. They were left holding a dirty rag.

I also needed to listen to faculty members in my department. Faculty members in our department felt unseen, misunderstood, and confused, and we needed to talk to each other. After all the negative publicity, we needed to discuss amongst ourselves who we were. I called a special meeting for our faculty members, held on Zoom, on July 7, 2021, the seventh day of my term. I offered four questions to anchor our discussion and circulated them before the meeting: "What have we learned about our department in the last two years?" "What have we been doing well that we want to keep doing?" "What have we been doing that we want to change?" and "What are our immediate next steps?"

There were a variety of responses to these questions. Some people said that they would never again attend any social events that included students. One person said that we should no longer have alcohol available at our holiday gathering. A couple of people thought we should admit fewer graduate students. One person talked about focusing our efforts on research, and one person said we should be open to preparing students for non-academic careers. One person spoke up for the introverts, saying that the emphasis on being a collegial department created pressure on people who get their best work done individually. The department as a whole had not been given any information about what concerns the administration had about our department, and that showed up in the responses to my questions. One person said, "Maybe we need an alternative to students and faculty socials, but I don't know what. Maybe that wasn't even the problem all along."

It was refreshing to be able to talk amongst ourselves, for people to be heard, to have a chance to listen, and to connect as a group. People talked about our care for our students and about our resilience. People suggested working to gain a better understanding of our students' points of view. Talking to each other and rebuilding trust was suggested as our next step. One colleague said, "Excellence in teaching and research will come after restoring trust and relationships." Their answers during that meeting helped me to formulate a plan to move forward.

The Inquiry and Remedy Committee

In normal times, being chair of an academic department is a full-time job, involving a lot of administrative tasks with annual deadlines, advocating on behalf of the department to those who hold power and resources, and mediating internal conversations. I had watched my predecessor's job become increasingly time-consuming as he simultaneously managed the usual activities of the department and tried to navigate the stress, confusion, and the massive operational interruption that resulted when department members were removed from their work.

My predecessor was involved in restructuring dozens of graduate supervisory committees and re-staffing multiple undergraduate courses that were vacated by faculty members put on administrative leaves, sometimes in the middle of the term. He became the supervisor of record for several of our stranded students. He also had to carefully manage communication within the department, with the upper administration, and with consultants who were hired by the university. I didn't think I could manage everything he had managed while learning and executing the normal tasks of a department chair.

Similarly, I would not have time to investigate the origins of the allegations and chair my department at the same time. How did one claim by one student become, over the course of several months, dozens of allegations against seven current and former department members? So, when I became chair in July of 2021, I created a new committee tasked with investigating how these events had come to pass and then making recommendations about improvements to policy and procedure to reduce the risk of a recurrence. I called this committee the Inquiry and Remedy Committee.

The first job of the Inquiry and Remedy Committee was to seek to understand what had happened. They studied minutes of the university's senate meetings and recent media coverage in the local news. They spoke to the students who had been in direct contact with the sexual violence intake office during the summer of 2020. The more they understood about the events of 2020, the more it became clear that the university administration needed this information. The committee believed that there had to be a university-wide investigation.

The details of what exactly happened in the summer of 2020 will not appear in this book. Those events are someone else's story to tell. This is a story about my job, as a transgender leader in academia, reintegrating people and using a values-based approach to get our department back to work.

All investigations and sanctions were organized above the department level. Although members of my department offered to liaise with a local sexual violence education group to organize trainings and to create a new alcohol policy, we were clearly told that such activities were not our prerogative and that the dean would organize a webinar for us about sexual harassment. I was just responsible for reintegrating people and setting the tone.

I know it may be frustrating to not understand the whole story. Imagine leading a large department without knowing what had happened behind closed doors. This feeling was ubiquitous my first two years as chair.

From Crisis to Clarity

In the weeks leading up to my becoming chair, I set some goals for myself. First, I had to assemble my team, which meant selecting three new associate chairs. One of my goals was "to lead people back to the research productivity and the excellence in research and teaching that they crave." The most challenging goal that I set was "We need to figure out how to communicate with our students so that they are not fearful."

Faculty supervisors were confused about what or how they were allowed to communicate to their students. Similarly, students were increasingly wary of communicating with faculty members and unsure whether rules had changed. As I came into office, the president had encouraged me to seek information from our students, but we did not have a coherent plan for delivering information to our students, even as our understanding of what had transpired was becoming clearer. I struggled with this communication for the first two years of my term.

On three occasions, my colleagues and I contemplated bringing all of our graduate students together for a big meeting to share information. First, I talked with my predecessor about convening a department-wide meeting for graduate students and providing an update. Another time, I talked with our graduate chair about organizing such a meeting. In each case, we ultimately decided that the potential to do harm to individual students or to our community was greater than our expected benefits. We were not entirely confident that we had the skill to manage the meeting if emotions flared, fear was foregrounded, or the discussion became difficult. Each time we contemplated bringing everyone together to discuss what had happened, we decided to let communication and healing progress organically instead.

Early in 2022, one graduate student voluntarily talked to every single student who was enrolled in our program—over 100 graduate students—and checked in with them. This particular student was known to be calm and empathetic. He was widely esteemed and universally trusted, so people were willing to talk to him. I trusted him. I knew him to be a person of integrity and compassion. From him, I learned that there was healing happening and that our graduate students were not afraid of the reintegration that was taking place. They were satisfied that those who had returned to work should be at work. My colleagues who had been returned to the workplace found this reassuring.

The graduate students themselves organized a meeting in March of 2022, and about 30 graduate students attended. Although faculty members did not attend that meeting, I heard from some of the students who attended. The newest students in our department were not scared, had positive feelings about the department, and were hopeful that in the future there would be social interactions between faculty members and students. Over time, the community was healing, and information was spreading.

In October of 2022, the university commissioned an external review of the university's DEI office, the office that had organized the allegations, interim measures, and investigations. Those external reviewers recommended "that senior administrators receive communication training on how to respond publicly to high stakes cases" (Andrews & Faure, 2023). This seemed like good advice, given the number of announcements that were made before any investigations had been completed. The external reviewers recommended that "All decisions pertaining to the office and its role need to be made in a manner befitting the ethical commitments of the institution and the transparency needed to rebuild trust and confidence, which may have been compromised due to a perceived lack of adherence to due process in the past," and furthermore, "Hiring decisions in the university need to be done in a transparent and consistent manner. The bar is even higher in this office." The university made this report public, and members of my department were beginning to understand that the processes followed had not been ideal.

Then came a real breakthrough. Early in 2023, Jonathan Kay, an investigative journalist from The Quillette, an online magazine that "focuses on long-form analysis and cultural commentary," started working on an article about what had happened to our department. Three of our graduate students talked to Kay, and those three students were among those who had direct contact with the university's sexual violence intake office in 2020. They told Kay what they had experienced and what they had witnessed. Finally, their story was important.

As Kay was doing his research, these students had the opportunity not just to tell their stories to him, but to talk to each other. In the summer of 2020, there was a lot of information that was confidential, and even the students at the epicenter of the storm had not heard each other's complete stories. Finally, these confidences were shared among our students. Kay published his story on June 14, 2023. We sat in the living room as Melanie read the 13,000-word article aloud. We both cried.

In addition to his long, investigative article, Jonathan Kay also published an article called "Lessons Learned." He concluded that conducting an investigation of every complaint might be a waste of time and an unnecessary interruption. "A university's own staff must retain the ability to reject or divert extremely dubious claims on a summary basis" (Kay, 2023). He concluded that there had to be independence of intake and investigation: "Having a single administrative worker manage both intake of sexual-violence complaints and subsequent case management is a bad idea." He drew attention to the severe and draconian nature of the posters and campus bans: "Interim disciplinary measures cause permanent damage." He also drew attention to the expense: "At least three separate law firms were able to enrich themselves... by performing investigative or consulting work associated with the sex-ring file and its fallout" (Kay, 2023).

Once the article was out, there was a lot of chatter on our grad students' Facebook page. Most people expressed that they were happy that the story was finally public. Some people were pleased that the article held the administration accountable. But after an 8-hour flurry, the chat reverted to more mundane topics. It appeared that the Quillette article, and the lively but brief communication that followed, was the closure our graduate students needed.

The atmosphere in the department changed palpably. Tension was released, and I felt relief. The article was going to make my job easier. Finally, there was a common understanding of what had transpired in 2020. Paradoxically, the Quillette article both gave us the freedom to talk about what happened and also the freedom to not talk about it. Some people in the department had felt morally compelled to advocate for our students and our department until somebody in power at the university listened, took the story seriously, and did something to increase safety on campus. Once published, we were confident that the story had been heard by the university's upper administration, senate, and board of governors. They would take an interest in making sure these events never recurred; we were confident. Relieved of this responsibility, we now had the freedom to not talk about these events.

At the same time, we also suddenly had the freedom to talk about everything that had happened, and its impact on our community. Many of the faculty members in the department had felt that we were being pressured to keep silent. While people were biting their tongues, there was an inequity across the department between people who knew what had happened and those who did not. Imagine entering our department as a new grad student or a new faculty member and realizing that there was something that everyone was whispering about but that no one would tell you about. Perhaps you have had the experience of entering a community with a proverbial elephant in its living room. It is hard to integrate into such a community. Now there is a story on the internet that can catch you up on this history in just 13,000 words.

The article mentioned me by name and described some of the struggles I had had while leading this maligned department. While in the role of chair, and because I was in that role, I had been careful not to make the story and the struggle about me. Still, I appreciated that the Quillette article acknowledged me. Months later I had an opportunity to visit The University of California at Santa Barbara and talk to some members of my former lab. They had read the article. They were impressed with my fortitude, and it felt good to know that my story, our story, was being read.

When Leading Is Advocacy

Where is the step-by-step playbook for leading an aggrieved organization? How do you care for the needs of people who have been harmed? How do you deescalate, care for those who have been wronged, and simultaneously preserve or repair the relationship with those in power? How do you negotiate a resolution? How was I going to advocate for my department?

Prior to my becoming chair, members of the department were angry at the university's administration for the negative publicity, for painting the entire department with a tarnished brush, and for the procedural irregularities that Jonathan Kay's investigation had uncovered. Before I became chair, dozens of faculty members filed two grievances against the president of the university, one of which I helped write. After I became chair, a third grievance was filed. Together with grievances submitted by individuals, there were a total of seven grievances filed against the university for the way they handled the allegations. The president of our faculty association commented "This has been a particularly challenging year, given the relatively larger number of investigations and grievances" (Hassini, 2021). There had been a total of four grievances in the previous 20 years. Working closely with some of my colleagues, I had to lead our department through the processes of making sure the university administration understood our concerns, created the necessary guardrails to prevent a recurrence, and then eventually repair our relationship with the administration. Leading my department through the resolution of our grievances was a leadership challenge that required especially careful communication.

As long as we were working to resolve our disagreements with the university, I felt that we needed to do so as a unified department, so it was crucial that I knew what the department wanted to do. It was my job to communicate with the department, both with those who had signed the grievances and with those who had not, as the grievances progressed to and through mediation. On the whole, members across the department shared a similar perspective on what had transpired and how. There was more diversity of opinion on what would be necessary in order to forgive the university's administration and therefore refocus our energy on our academic mission. I had to balance the needs of those who could never forgive (faculty members whose students had been directly harmed) with the desires of those who wanted to get back to work, and with the perspective of those who thought that any engagement with the upper administration, where all the power, money, and legal resources sit, was dangerous. Some wanted money. Some wanted a public apology. Some wanted an explanation. Some just wanted the president and provost to walk across campus to sit down and listen to us.

How long do we continue to try to have dialogue? When do we stand down? It was my role to listen deeply and then to reflect back to the department about what we were willing to insist upon, and when we were going to turn our attention to repairing our relationship with the university. My job started with listening and hearing what everybody was thinking and, just as importantly, creating opportunities for everyone to hear each other.

I had to balance what I was hearing.

The process was surprisingly protracted. We were over a year and a half into my term as chair when a day-long mediation session was scheduled to resolve our grievances. Ahead of the mediation sessions, I held several meetings with the faculty members who had signed the grievances and followed each mediation session with a detailed summary because I needed ongoing, open communication in order to continually keep myself and the department apprised of everyone's viewpoint.

By the time I had completed my second year as chair, we had mediated a resolution to the three departmental grievances. We had come to a point where there was a widespread understanding about how the events of 2020 had come about. The Inquiry and Remedy Committee had come to understand some of the behind-the-scenes decisions that had been made prior to and during the summer of 2020. The Quillette article had been accessed by hundreds of thousands of people according to an online tally, and a university-sponsored investigation into the events of 2020 was underway. Working together as a department we had succeeded in ensuring that the university administration knew what had happened to our students in the summer of 2020 by advocating for an investigation. I thought we were at a point where we, as a department, could stand down. We could end our conflict with the upper administration and rebuild a relationship. My next step was to figure out how to navigate that.

In July of 2023, I was considering telling the department at our monthly departmental meeting that we were done advocating for further investigations and repair. As the meeting approached, I talked to colleagues who had been in leadership in the department in 2020. I talked to my colleagues who had been most intimately impacted and to colleagues whose students had been impacted so that they knew ahead of the meeting that I was considering telling the department that we were moving on. I had to take the temperature of the whole department, to understand where there was still anger, where there was healing, and where there was an appetite to rebuild. I reached out to the people who were still struggling to forgive. I wanted them to hear my intentions before the meeting, and I wanted them to hear why I was thinking it was time to move on. They let me know that they understood why we had come to the appropriate time for the department to stand down.

I started the faculty meeting with an agenda item I called "Reflections on my first two years as chair." I shared with the faculty and staff gathered at the meeting the goals that I had set for myself when I became chair. I told them that the most challenging goal was communicating with our graduate students. I shared that I was hearing from our graduate students that the Quillette article and their chat after it came out was the closure they needed. I summarized the accomplishments of the Inquiry & Remedy committee, including the upcoming investigation. Then I told my colleagues that "the work that we needed to do together as a department is done." There was applause and there were tears.

The Flaherty Report

The Inquiry and Remedy Committee successfully advocated for an investigation into the policies and processes that led to the events of 2020. The investigation was conducted by Michelle Flaherty, at the time a labor arbitrator, mediator, and independent investigator. The upper administration and our faculty association collaborated to design and commission this investigation. On May 2, 2023, the university announced the launch of this investigation: "Community input sought as part of ongoing review of university policies." Many people in our department participated in the investigation, which ultimately resulted in the 100-plus page Flaherty Report that recommended best practices for managing allegations and investigation. A summary of the document was shared publicly on July 5, 2024. Flaherty pointed to many of the same lessons that Jonathan Kay had, but now the university had those suggestions in a report that they themselves had commissioned. This important document recommends best practices that could be useful not just at our university but for universities across the world. This is a brief summary of Flaherty's recommendations.

Although it was the practice of the university to conduct investigations in any case where the allegations would be a policy violation, Flaherty recommended exceptions to this rule when allegations were "patently ridiculous or incapable of proof" or "a person who had been accused of wrongdoing had clear evidence that they were not in the place where the alleged offense was supposed to have occurred" (Andrews, 2025, p. 9). These exceptions could save time, money, and disruptive upheaval in the workplace.

The Flaherty Report suggested that it was important for the person whose job it is to hear complaints and concerns "to be, and seen to be, 'scrupulously neutral'" (Andrews, 2025, p. 6) and "that a separate complaint-handling office be created to enhance impartiality and procedural fairness" and to ensure a neutral and unbiased investigation (Andrews, 2025, p. 14). Specifically, Flaherty recommended "that a bright line of separation be kept between complaint intake staff and support staff" (Andrews, 2025, p. 8). The intake staff was the person responsible for taking the complaints. Flaherty went on to say, "in the past, some intake staff viewed their role as advocating for complainants and assisting in making complaints more robust" (Andrews, 2025, p. 6) and therefore consulted with potential complainants in order to build "stronger" cases. The Flaherty Report recommended that "intake offices should not play any role in support or advocacy" (Andrews, 2025, p. 3).

The report recommended "procedural fairness." The report emphasized that intake and investigation processes need to be "impartial" and that decision makers also needed to be "impartial." The Flaherty Report said that the university needs to be "more transparent, fair, and supportive" (Andrews, 2025, p. 13).

The Flaherty Report commented on the distribution of posters with the accused photo and name, concurrent with their being banned from campus. She called this "one of the most serious interim measures that can be imposed on a respondent. In the context of balancing competing interests, including the university's interests in protecting its reputation," Flaherty recommended that "the university review whether it can protect safety and reputation with interim measures that are less harmful to the respondent" (Andrews, 2025, p. 13). She said, "it is crucial to consider whether other less severe measures can address safety concerns" (Andrews, 2025, p. 19). The Flaherty Report recommended that the university "should make it clear that interim measures are not disciplinary in nature and not evidence of misconduct" (Andrews, 2025, p. 18). Relatedly, the report noted that the university has obligations to confidentiality and noted the tension that occurs if the university makes public comments while the accused are prevented by obligations to confidentiality from publicly responding.

The Flaherty Report was clear that people who were accused should be told what they were accused of: "once the decision to investigate has been made, and at all stages thereafter, respondents have the right to know the allegations against them and the opportunity to respond to them" (Andrews, 2025, p. 4).

Finally, the Flaherty Report recommended that the university "systematically explore restorative measures at the close of the investigation process" (Andrews, 2025). I read that and wondered how my job would have been different if someone had contemplated the restoration of the department while decisions were being made in the summer of 2020. As they removed people from work, circulated posters, and announced the department's complacency, how did they think anyone could repair the department?

The university is currently working on implementing these suggestions.

Back to Work

We had been moving toward getting back to work for my entire term as chair. Through the grievance process, the external review of the DEI office, the Quillette articles, and finally the Flaherty Report, we had achieved so much.

Communication was the key to getting back to work. This communication was not achieved in one conversation. This communication took years of deliberate, intentional, and reiterative talking and listening. I was glad that we had worked hard at listening to each other and that we were able to, if not completely heal, at least put the crisis behind us and get back to work. What we achieved, we achieved together through the work of the Inquiry and Remedy Committee, our associate chairs, my predecessor, past department chairs, and my senior colleagues. I had faced a tremendous communication challenge when I became chair, a challenge that I had no preparation for. I don't think anyone had really contemplated how one could navigate what our department had to get through in order to rebuild trust and get back to work. If I had to do it again, I would be more insistent that I needed support from the upper administration. I was such a rookie when I had that first meeting with the president.

Discovering the origins of our crisis and communicating what we learned both within the department and to the university's administration was precarious and formidable, but there was more to do. Working together in collaboration heals relationships and heals communities. We were going to work together to build a department based on our shared values.

References

Adolphs, R. (2013). The biology of fear. *Current Biology, 23*(2), R79–R93. https://doi.org/10.1016/j.cub.2012.11.055

Andrews, P. (2025). President's report: Reflections on university investigation processes. https://macfaculty.mcmaster.ca/app/uploads/2025/04/MUFA-Presidents-Report-Reflections-on-university-investigation-processes.pdf

Andrews, P., & Faure, P. (2023). Equity and inclusion requires accountability and transparency. https://macfaculty.mcmaster.ca/app/uploads/2023/03/202303Newsletter.pdf

Brown, B. (2018). *Dare to lead: Brave work. Tough conversations. Whole hearts.*

De Ridder, J. (2021). Deep disagreements and political polarization. In E. Edenberg & M. Hannon (Eds.), *Political epistemology* (pp. 226–243). Oxford University Press. https://doi.org/10.1093/oso/9780192893338.003.0013

Hassini, E. (2021). President's Report. https://macfaculty.mcmaster.ca/app/uploads/2021/05/202105Newsletter.pdf

Jane, E. A. (2014). "Back to the kitchen, cunt": Speaking the unspeakable about online misogyny. *Continuum, 28*(4), 558–570. https://doi.org/10.1080/10304312.2014.924479

Kay, J (2023). Lessons from an academic social panic. https://quillette.com/blog/2023/06/18/lessons-from-mcmaster-universitys-2020-sex-ring-social-panic/

Lerner, M., & Simmons, C. H. (1966). Observer's reaction to the 'innocent victim': Compassion or rejection? *Journal of Personality and Social Psychology, 4*(2), 203–210. https://doi.org/10.1037/h0023562. PMID 5969146

Nagata, J. M., Balasubramanian, P., Diep, T., Ganson, K. T., Testa, A., He, J., & Baker, F. C. (2025). Cyberbullying victimization among transgender and gender-questioning early adolescents. *Academic Pediatrics, 25*(3), 102624. https://doi.org/10.1016/j.acap.2024.102624

Posselt, J., Reyes, K. A., Slay, K. E., Kamimura, A., & Porter, K. B. (2017). Equity efforts as boundary work: How symbolic and social boundaries shape access and inclusion in graduate education. *Teachers College Record, 119*(10), 1–38. https://doi.org/10.1177/016146811711901003

Roser, M. E., & Gazzaniga, M. S. (2006). The interpreter in human psychology. In J. H. Kaas (Ed.), *The evolution of primate nervous systems* (pp. 191–200). Elsevier.

Rutherford, M. D. (2004). The effect of social role on theory of mind reasoning. *British Journal of Psychology, 95*(1), 91–103. https://doi.org/10.1348/000712604322779488

4

Values-Based Governance

I stepped into this role knowing that it would be difficult. My department was in distress, and it needed to be led with care and compassion. I needed an action plan, and I needed it right away. I put a lot of effort into communication and to really listening, but I also felt that the healing process would be enhanced by anchoring our activities in our shared values. Articulating my values and then my department's values could be the foundation for a roadmap out of the mire. The benefit of articulating your values is that you have some mooring, some principles that you can refer to any time you make a challenging decision. This applies to both the strategic decisions that you have time to ponder and the pressing decisions that you make several times a day.

The university's administration was not offering any guidance, sympathy, or information, but I wasn't on my own. During my first year, people stopped by my office everyday to check in with me, to share their experiences with me, and to talk to me about how we were going to rebuild. My department was ready to do the work of building values-based governance. Working together as a department to articulate our values would create an opportunity for people to listen to each other and to work together. And I had Gail.

Naming My Personal Values

During my first two years as chair, I had regular, near-weekly conversations with Gail, a former school principal and a leadership coach. She has a lot of experience in values-based leadership, and she helped me develop the values-based governance that I relied on to lead my department's recovery.

We always met on Zoom, I in the chair's office, she in her dining room. She sometimes looked like she'd just delivered a talk, and she sometimes looked like she'd just been gardening, but she was always ready to engage in my challenges and opportunities.

She helped me make sense of the chaos that I was trying to quell. She gave me very practical advice about how to lead effectively and how to avoid falling into the trap of managing rather than leading. Gail reminded me that when my superiors were acting angry or unpredictable, my best strategy was to continue to be collaborative and transparent. She helped me create the space for healing.

We started by doing the work of articulating my personal values. Gail explained that while there are a lot of values that are important and useful, it's best to prioritize two or three. You start by listing up to ten values that resonate with you. Next make sure you know what you mean by each value on your list. For example, if "respect" is on your list, are you clear on whether you intend to treat others with respect or whether you will demand others treat you with respect? Be clear on how each value could be enacted. Then rank your list in order of which value would be most relevant given your current context.

Working through this process, the two values I centered were compassion and integrity. After watching the events of the previous year and a half unfold, it was clear to me that people across the department needed compassion. Lives had been disrupted and destroyed when draconian interim measures were imposed before any investigations were complete. People had been cut off from communicating, and "Wanted Ad" style posters were circulated with their photos and names. Some people were left scared about what dangers might be lurking in our community. The entire department was tender. They needed compassion badly.

The department was also desperate for a leader with integrity. There had been a lot of misinformation swirling about. Students had very publicly asked the university president to share the results of investigations: "An understanding of the situation is needed so that we can make our own informed decisions about how to keep ourselves safe in the workplace. Increased communication would benefit all parties involved, rather than relying on rumours and hearsay." Students went on to critique the university's recent public communication: "assaults are not due to 'lack of boundaries' or 'alcohol'," so our students were clear that those "should not be the focus of the plan of action." People needed a leader who could sort through the misinformation and biased communication to provide some insight into what was actually happening. My department needed clarity and integrity.

I kept compassion and integrity in focus throughout my five-year term.

Once I had articulated the values I would be prioritizing, Gail made me articulate a measurable standard. She asked, "How will you know that you are living this value? What are the benchmarks to measure against?" I wrote down answers, which would serve to guide me throughout my term. I wrote, "When people have made a mistake, I will treat them with compassion, helping them learn and make a path forward." I said that the department would "Get our work done with each other, listening deeply, and assuming good intent" and that together we would "Heal from the betrayal by the university, reestablishing trust." Looking back on these standards, they seem ambitious.

With explicit values central to my leadership, my responses to the onslaught of daily decisions became well-practiced over time. My values became easy to access, and comparing my next move to those values became nearly automatic. In addition to me articulating my personal values that would guide me during my term as chair, it was important for our department to collectively identify the values that would underlie our governance. Our department had started the process of defining our core values before we were delayed by COVID-19. Now we needed to come together to create our statement of the values we wanted to use in our own governance. Not so fast.

Values Delayed

The cornerstone of values-based governance is the values that are created and held jointly by an organization. I was personally eager to get to work articulating our core values because I wanted to use values-based governance to get our department back on track. Being clear and explicit regarding our shared values was expected to be a foundation for many types of decisions that we make as a group. When we decide what new faculty positions we are going to advertise, update our curriculum, populate our committees, or design an expansion of our building, we want agreed-upon values and principles so that we know the purpose of our activities. And I wanted to use formal consensus decision-making, which requires that a group have explicit shared values.

The faculty and students in our department were eager to get together and discuss the values that we shared. The negative publicity that our department had endured conflicted with our self-perception. Our sense of self had been challenged, and we were desperate to connect to reaffirm who we thought we were. It was time to create an explicit statement that articulated our shared values to serve as the cornerstone of our procedures and governance.

Before I became department chair, our department had gathered in a faculty retreat in December of 2019 to start naming our values. We didn't have a professional facilitator, and the retreat included just our 30 faculty members—we made no attempt to reach out to students, postdocs, or staff. We brainstormed a list of values, wrote them on a whiteboard, and photographed the whiteboard. That was it. We did not finalize our core values statement. We really weren't even sure what our process was, or how other organizations had created their core values statements.

Of course, we knew that this was a preliminary step. We intended to return to the project, but we had no idea what lay ahead. Both the pandemic and the publicity around the allegations disrupted our work for much longer than any of us could have foreseen. For many months, our attention was pulled elsewhere. When we tried to return to the project of creating our core values, we were delayed because we did not yet have my supervisor's permission to discuss our values.

It was the chair of our DEI committee who tried to return us to our core values exercise. She had been at our December 2019 faculty retreat and believed strongly that creating a core values statement was our next step in supporting our culture of inclusion and caring. I whole-heartedly supported her.

I checked in with my supervisor—I'll call her The Supervisor. At the time, I didn't think of it as asking permission—no department had ever been forbidden from talking about their values—but I was new, and I didn't want any missteps as we built our relationship, so I emailed her:

> Our department DEI committee would like to organize a core values exercise for our department, designed to identify the values that anchor our department's decisions and activities. This exercise was originally planned before the COVID-19 shutdown but was delayed. The DEI committee has picked up this idea and has interviewed facilitators who do this sort of work. ... I wanted to check with you before they proceed.

Nope. I was told, "I do not support you moving forward with [the core values exercise] in August...." She wanted us to complete some webinar training before we talked about our core values. She was in conversations with Alan Berkowitz, an independent consultant in Northern California "who helps colleges, universities, and communities design programs that address health and social justice issues," according to his website. She told me, "I am bringing forward a comprehensive training and education plan as directed by the President and Provost and in response to the events of the last year." She went on to say, "The training and education are meant to provide a common foundation of language and knowledge which I believe will then assist the DEI committee in advancing the core values exercise." Then she went on vacation. I had counted on some serious and thoughtful support. Was I going to have to navigate this situation without support from The Supervisor?

Members of my department were surprised that we were not yet allowed to discuss our core values. None of us had ever heard of a department being told they couldn't discuss their values. One senior member of our department told me that I should stop informing The Supervisor of our activities. Still, several people in the department thought it was important that we try to smooth our relationship with her, so we canceled our plans to pick up the discussion we had started prior to the shutdown. In December, the webinars, custom made for our department, were delivered to us via Zoom.

Our DEI chair again asked the dean for permission to discuss our core values as a department. We finally received The Supervisor's permission "to move forward with your core values exercise in early 2022." We began to discuss our core values in January of 2022.

Identifying Our Core Values

We wanted to have a broad conversation across the entire department, and we had never organized such an exercise before. We were 30 faculty members, 20 staff, 10 postdocs, 110 graduate students, and about 1300 undergraduate students. We needed to use a process that would allow us to articulate our commonly held values across this large group of people who share a common academic purpose. The department hired Darlene Chrissley, a change consultant, leadership coach, and learning facilitator. She had experience with guiding organizations in articulating their core values. She endorsed our belief that articulating our values could strengthen our organization's culture. The right values might help you optimize the processes of your organization and move you toward the mission of the organization. Of course, in academia, our mission is research and teaching, while in a business the mission might be to maximize profit.

Darlene gave us some assigned readings and we learned Shalom H. Schwartz's values framework. He describes 10 universal human values, with a relationship that can be depicted by placing them around a ring. These shared values make social interaction possible (Schwartz, 2012).

The exercise started with four large group meetings: faculty, staff and postdoc, graduate students, and undergraduate students. This was during a term when classes were moving back into the classroom, and some of our meetings took place in person while everyone wore masks and a new air purifier hummed in the corner of the room. We brainstormed a large list of our own personal values (for example, we named respect, integrity, compassion, and security). Faculty members nominated respect, integrity, and compassion. Graduate students nominated achievement, learning, and problem-solving. Staff nominated achievement, self-direction, and security. Our undergraduates nominated empathy, honesty, and respect. Clearly, we needed to be gathering all of these perspectives in order to understand the values in the department.

Each group then met to further discuss the values they had nominated. Darlene helped us categorize what we were naming, based on Schwartz's universal human values, and then helped us to rank them. Of Schwartz's 10 universal values (power, achievement, hedonism, stimulation, self-direction, universalism, benevolence, tradition, conformity, and security), our group of faculty members ranked self-direction and achievement highest, and conformity lowest.

We circulated the categorized and ranked results from each group meeting, so everyone could see what students, staff, postdocs, and faculty valued. Some values were repeated often, like Compassion, Respect, Transparency, and Perspective-Taking. We considered all of the suggestions and noticed what values were most common. As we contemplated what we valued, we realized that our values might differ based on context—for example, whether we were engaged in research, teaching, decision-making, or conflict resolution. We created a ranked list of values for each of those domains.

Representatives from each group then met and our discussion was again facilitated by Darlene. We had a lot of agreement and took great care to listen to minority voices—people who were advocating for a value that hadn't appeared frequently. We wanted to make sure we understood why such a value was important to our colleague.

I found it remarkable to have undergraduate students discussing departmental governance with faculty, staff, postdocs, and graduate students. We had never invited undergraduates into governance conversations before, and their presence was meaningful. In fact, it was an undergraduate representative who insisted that we include the word "safe" in our core values, and I was very pleased when this value ended up in our draft.

We circulated our draft to the entire department:

Our Community is:
> Compassionate, Kind, and Supportive
> Safe, Inclusive, and Respectful
> Transparent, Accountable, and Empowering

We engage in Research and Scholarship with:
> Curiosity, Integrity, and Inclusive Collaboration

In Teaching and Learning we value:
> Excellence, Fairness, and Fun

Our Decision-Making is:
> Evidence-Based, Consensus-Driven, and Thoughtful

We approach conflict resolution with:
> Open-mindedness, Perspective-Taking, and Respect

We asked for specific feedback:

1) To what extent does this statement reflect the core values that we as a community aspire to live by?
2) Is there anything that you find unclear or confusing?
3) Is there anything that is critical but missing from this statement?

People sent in suggestions. A staff person proposed, "I would suggest adding something like a firm expectation or demand for rigor in research." A faculty member wrote, "The teaching and learning one is rather generic and could perhaps be beefed up a bit. What does "excellence" mean here, specifically? Why would we strive for anything less than that?" and another faculty member also wrote, "I dislike the word "excellence" because it doesn't seem like something we can tie metrics to. What is our plan to achieve 'excellence'?" Yet another faculty member commented, "We have the word "respectful" and "respect" in two places. I think we should remove it from one place and replace it with a different word to broaden impact."

Lastly, the representatives of each group met again to incorporate feedback on the draft. We settled on this statement:

Our community is:
    Compassionate, Kind, and Supportive
    Safe, Inclusive, and Courteous
    Transparent, Accountable, and Empowering
We engage in research and scholarship with:
    Curiosity, Rigor, and Inclusive Collaboration
In teaching and learning we value:
    Critical Thinking, Fairness, and Fun
Our decision-making is:
    Evidence-Based, Consensus-Driven, and Thoughtful
We approach conflict resolution with:
    Open-mindedness, Perspective-Taking, and Respect

It was healing for the department to engage in such a positive discussion together. We were communicating with each other, and we were claiming the prerogative to define ourselves and our values. It was refreshing to be in control of how we were defined after we had read such scathing characterizations of our department, including from our own president, in the local news. Our values have become part of the fabric of the department.

Values in Action

Gail advised me to keep our values visible. She told me, "Never miss an opportunity to reinforce the values that are the foundation of your culture." An undergraduate with some graphic design skills created a visually appealing poster, and we displayed our new core values statement all over the building. Whenever I had an opportunity to speak to the department, at our graduate research day, our undergraduate-organized neuroscience conference, or at our welcome day each

September, I always took the opportunity to name our values. Every time a new staff member joined our department, I met with them individually, told them about our core values process, and gave them the poster.

Now that our values were explicit, widely circulated, and posted throughout our building, we were ready to start governing using these values. We wanted our activities to be consistent with our values. I wanted to conduct a gap analysis to align our standard operating procedures with our values, and I wanted to practice formal consensus decision-making. We got to work.

The first thing I did was to create a document called "This is how we do it" in order to document our practices. Our department has never had bylaws. Creating bylaws can be a lengthy and contentious process, especially if the group is engaged and conscientious enough to put some effort into brainstorming unintended consequences. The more possible outcomes you imagine, the longer your document gets.

Enforcing bylaws can be a contentious process as well. Once a disagreement arises, people will have positional perspectives and will interpret bylaws in ways that advantage their position. Furthermore, it is impossible to anticipate every eventuality from budget challenges to challenging personalities, so no set of bylaws guarantees a smooth road ahead.

Our "This is how we do it" document includes this preamble:

> The department does not have bylaws. Instead, we have this document describing how our practices and procedures are consistent with our core values. This document is descriptive, not proscriptive. It describes how we get things done but does not dictate how we get things done. This is a Living Document: it can be modified, updated, or overhauled if the department feels that different procedures better match our core values. This document has undergone a Gap Analysis and can do so again if questions arise. Ideally, this document will serve to help new department members and new department leaders participate in our processes.

This is essentially a standard operating procedure document that describes but does not dictate how we get things done. It describes how we evaluate faculty performance for salary increases, how we mentor graduate students, how we allocate TAs, and how we decide what area of research we want to bolster next time we have an opportunity to hire a faculty member, for example, and it describes the duties of the chair and associate chairs.

This document allows new department members and leaders to understand our processes well enough to participate in them. I recently attended a meeting of another organization on campus in which a member made a constructive suggestion, but when the chair invited her to "make a motion" she said, "Oh, no. I've never made a motion. I don't understand the process well enough." A good road map to your processes paves the way to participation.

It is a living document, but updates are not completely unconstrained. Updates must be values-driven, and the process we use to update the document is a gap analysis. The second thing I did on the road to values-based governance was to lead a gap analysis. Very shortly after we had finished our core values document, we conducted a gap analysis during a departmental retreat, on a sunny spring day at a conference venue at a marina overlooking our local bay. Unlike our previous faculty retreats, we did not employ a facilitator. Gail told me that my department needed to see me at the front of the room, so I facilitated the day-long retreat.

We sat at six tables in groups of 5 or 6, and I had assigned the seating so that every table had a group representative of faculty and staff, junior and senior department members, teaching and research faculty, and experts in a variety of subdisciplines. Each group received a copy of our core values and one topic from the "This is how we do it" document. I invited people to directly compare our processes to our values and notice any inconsistencies. Each group discussed whether our standard practices, as described in the document, matched our core values. Participants could discuss amongst themselves and then write comments or edits directly on the pages of the document. Next, I facilitated a larger discussion of each section, making notes on a flip chart so everyone could see.

Following the retreat, I updated our document. For example, we added detail to our strategic planning guidelines, stating explicitly that the planning committee is populated "following principles of equity, representation, leadership development, and succession planning." We added "The Strategic Planning committee will create a process that allows for broad input. The resulting plan should include considerations from all faculty members." We elaborated the section describing consensus decision-making by adding "This process is unhurried, especially as the group approaches consensus. It is important that careful minutes are taken so that dissenting concerns can be used in developing the proposal," and a paragraph was added offering strategies for including all of the voices in the decision, even if people feel shy or intimidated during a meeting. "For example, input could be gathered using an electronic poll before or during a meeting. One could schedule a private meeting for people to talk among themselves and present a summary of their discussion to the larger group."

The document was then circulated to staff and faculty for further comment. We now operate with the document that resulted from this gap analysis, and at any time, we can consider whether our practices are consistent with our core values. Anyone in the department can propose a gap analysis and, if they want to, can point us to a specific process and a specific value that they want us to compare.

Formal Consensus Decision-Making

Recently, I was struck by the struggles of leading without a foundation of values when I attended a leadership workshop on campus. An external consultant had been hired to talk to us about change management. Since the workshop was on a university campus and presented to academic leaders, she was talking to us about implementing change in an academic context. The speaker's approach to change management involved her telling us about the resistance we were going to meet. She told us we had to move forward and move people through change, despite this resistance, and despite any creative ideas they might offer to take a different direction. The conversation seemed foreign to me. Since I don't try to implement decisions that people don't want to implement, I don't have to deal with such situations.

The consultant told us that 20% of people aren't going to want to implement a change that leaders want to make. I wondered about the wisdom of proceeding with a plan that a fifth of your people don't want to do. It is very likely that your team is full of smart people. If I were getting resistance to a decision, I would get curious about why my team was resisting the change. I would explain the original problem that I was trying to solve and enroll them in the task of constructing a solution that works for everyone. Even if I was unable to come up with the solution on my own, I'm pretty sure the group would have some creative ideas. Those are the kinds of ideas that emerge when a group uses a consensus decision-making process.

Consensus decision-making has a deep history, and the tradition I am familiar with comes from the Quakers. In Quaker communities, decisions are not made by voting, but by "communal discernment" during which everyone listens for the truth that emerges when you leave space for everyone to speak. Everyone has some wisdom to offer based on their values and lived experience, and you haven't finished listening until you have made space for every voice. It is a slow and quiet process.

The fifth of the eight Unitarian Universalist principles is "The right of conscience and the use of the democratic process within our congregations and in society at large." People should have a voice when decisions are being made that will impact them. It was in the UU community that I learned why and how to use consensus decision-making.

I was first introduced to consensus decision-making in the summer of 2001. Melanie and I had gotten involved in the continent-wide young adults' organization through the Jefferson Unitarian Church in Golden, Colorado. I was invited to moderate a business meeting, which would take place at Unirondack, a UU camp located in the Adirondack Mountains of upstate New York. We all cooked together and had chores we had to perform. Because I was moderating the business meeting and because this group used formal consensus to make their decisions, I was trained in the process by Kevin, a young adult who had grown up in the Quaker tradition.

In Quaker communities, consensus decision-making is part of the culture, so people don't need to learn the process explicitly. They have witnessed it their whole lives. The consensus process that I learned was formalized by a group called "Food not Bombs," a non-violent organization, founded in 1980, that recovers food that would otherwise be discarded and shares free meals with the people who need that food. Formal consensus decision-making makes this process teachable by naming the roles and stages of the process so that people who haven't practiced it before can participate. The process struck me as powerful, compassionate, creative, fair, and equitable. I could use such a process to get my department back on track. Not only could we salvage the department, we could learn a better way of being together.

With our core values statement in hand, we were ready to start using formal consensus decision-making. I led a workshop at a faculty meeting that introduced the goals and practices of formal consensus decision-making. I explained the values, the history, and the intentions. When a group is using formal consensus decision-making, the proposal belongs to the group, not the presenter, and the group can modify it as they wish. Ideally the proposal should be shared in advance of the meeting so that people have time to contemplate whether they have any concerns or suggestions.

Formal consensus decision-making is an inherently values-based process because objections to any proposal must be related to the explicit values, goals, or principles of the group. People are then free to raise concerns about the proposal, but the concern has to be rooted in the group's values. If someone suggests a concern ("That doesn't sit well with me," "The person who made that proposal didn't support the last proposal I made," or "Let's hire my nephew instead"), the group is free to decide that the concern is not values-based and move on.

No proposal is adopted until all concerns are dealt with one way or another. The moderator must take great care to be sure that all concerns have been heard before declaring that consensus has been reached. The last few minutes as the group approaches consensus are slow because the moderator leaves time for someone to gather their thoughts and articulate a concern. The moderator states that it appears that the group is approaching consensus, asks if there are any more concerns, and then leaves a pause long enough that they'll probably start feeling awkward. Then they declare that consensus has been reached.

Usually, the group figures out a way to incorporate each concern while preserving the intent of the original proposal, and consensus is reached. Sometimes people do stand aside, allowing the proposal to be accepted by the group despite an unresolved concern, but in my experience, that doesn't happen until they believe that their colleagues listened to and understood their concern. The process becomes easier as the group becomes more practiced, and people learn to trust that their voices will be heard. Practicing consensus decision-making has had a lasting impact on our department's culture: people trust that they will be heard and trust that their perspective will be valued. Meetings have taken on a more tranquil pace.

Teaching the values, the goals, and the process around formal consensus decision-making is often enough to create a culture where people are committed to hearing every concern before a decision is made. That is to say, you don't actually have to take that scary last step of deciding (by formal consensus) that the only decision-making process you'll ever use is formal consensus. Our department never took that step, but in my entire term as chair, we never voted unless a vote was required by policy.

Years ago, Melanie and I delivered our formal consensus workshop to a group of parents who were working together to support an alternative school. After teaching them the process, we led them through a demonstration, and the proposal that they used for the demonstration was "We will use formal consensus decision making to make all of our decisions." The next thirty or so minutes unfolded as expected: people spoke in favor, people raised concerns, and people elaborated on the original proposal in order to incorporate solutions to the concerns. The meeting was scheduled to end at 9 o'clock, and as the hour approached, the group seemed to be moving toward consensus. Excitement was in the air. The group was on the verge of adopting a decision-making process. But remember, the moments when the group approaches consensus must be handled slowly. Before the moderator declares that consensus has been reached, they have to leave enough silence for a dissenting voice to weigh in unhurriedly.

As the moderator, I said that we were moving toward consensus. I asked if there were any unheard concerns. With mere seconds left until the end of the meeting, a parent said, "Wait, we can't really do this! We'll be stymied! Nothing will get done if we can only make decisions by consensus." I, as moderator of our demonstration, said, "It is nine o'clock, we have not reached consensus, and the meeting is adjourned. We learned two things: (1) Consensus decision-making favors the status quo. If you don't reach consensus, you revert to existing processes. (2) It didn't really matter. Now this group knew how to listen to all of the voices in the room before they voted. Making that intention explicit is usually enough to impact your culture.

The Original Blueprint

Formal consensus decision-making is a steady, deliberate, and creative process. Much of the time during a meeting is spent considering the concerns that are brought forward. Once every concern and viewpoint are built into the solution, the result is a plan that is creative, inclusive, and has broad agreement.

In addition to making space for every voice, another advantage to consensus decision-making is that you get everyone's "buy-in," which leads to greater participation. If we have to decide whether we are going to build a bridge and ten people vote yes and seven people vote no, the majority has won, but they still might not get their bridge. The people who voted "no" are unlikely to show up when it comes time to put in the work to build the bridge. If you want to move a new project forward, you need your group to support it. Making sure everyone is contributing to the decision enrolls them in the project. The most important times to use such a robust decision-making process are if the decision is going to be controversial or if the successful implementation of the decision relies on enthusiastic acceptance.

The best resource I've found on the topic is a book called *On Conflict and Consensus* by C.T. Lawrence Butler and Amy Rothstein, available from Food Not Bombs Publishing. After I published an article on my department's use of consensus—"Consensus decision-making is surprisingly effective in both communities and workplaces"—in The Conversation, a website that publishes news and research written by academics, C.T. Lawrence Butler mailed me the third edition of the book. I was surprised to hear from the author of this resource, which I had been using for decades. In a follow-up email, C.T. explained that

> Consensus is a decision-making process that is based on values. In voting, one amasses enough power to win the vote; in consensus, the group, a priori, identifies and defines the group's purpose and commonly held values and makes decisions based on how closely the proposal matches the defined purpose and values; if it matches, it is adopted, even if only one member wants it. If it doesn't match, it is rejected or amended, regardless of how many members want it.

I was pretty excited to hear from Butler. Our views on the reasons to use consensus matched, and my faith in the process was affirmed. Formal consensus decision-making is an intentionally inclusive process that ensures that everyone is heard, and every point of view is incorporated into the proposal or project. This contrasts with the practice of majority-rule voting. Perhaps you have been in a meeting that has started to become heated. People are becoming positional and perhaps afraid that their view will not prevail. Suddenly someone who holds the majority viewpoint shouts out "Let's vote" and the opportunity to contribute a dissenting opinion has ended. Voting prevents the minority voices from participating in ongoing discussion.

Within the department, these goals of the process were appreciated. One junior faculty member said of me, "I've also sat in many different committees that he chaired, and he has always pushed for establishing proper processes and following them, and also made efforts to include every departmental stakeholder at multiple time points whenever decisions were being made."

Consensus in Action

We had posted a position for a new faculty member, and when two outstanding candidates rose to the top of our list, the hiring committee did not reach consensus immediately. The two candidates were at different stages in their career, so a direct comparison was impossible. Instead, we used our consensus process to create a solution that suited everyone. We asked for the funding to hire both and delegated two committee members to bring this proposal forward for consideration. We were able to hire both of these strong academics. Had we not been using consensus decision-making, we would have voted and hired whichever candidate had the most votes.

On two different occasions, other hiring committees had trouble coming to consensus. Members of the committee had different preferred candidates. Again, had we not been using consensus decision-making, we would have voted, and the candidate with the most votes would have been hired. Moreover, the person with the dissenting opinion would have been silenced, and their concerns would not have been incorporated into our final decision. Instead, we listened to the concerns of our dissenting colleague and created a solution to address the concerns, which was to devise a specific support plan for the new staff person that was tailored to address the concerns that had been expressed. Fundamentally, the magic of consensus decision-making is that it is a creative process.

I was both pleased and surprised by these outcomes. When I learned formal consensus, I was taught that there were certain decisions that did not lend themselves to consensus decision-making because it was hard to find creative solutions that address everyone's concerns. If you were choosing a paint color, consensus would be difficult because if some people want blue and some people want yellow, there isn't a creative way to meet everyone's needs. I was also taught that the selection of an individual (e.g., hiring) wasn't suited to consensus because you can't take the attractive characteristics of candidate A and mix them with the attractive characteristics of candidate B. You might as well vote. So, the creative outcomes that arose in the context of hiring astonished even me. The process was even more powerful than I expected.

Consensus decision-making has supported the collaborative culture of our department as people have come to trust that all voices will be heard. We don't have business meetings in which people feel they have to be loud or fast in order to be heard. Our meetings are largely calm and tend to be collegial. This kind of community-based decision-making is deeply fulfilling. Over time, people get more adept at using this process.

Building Culture with Values

If you center your leadership on your values, those values can be the foundation of your daily decisions and of the processes that you implement and rely on over time. Without that foundation, it is easy to drift into expediency and efficiency, until you eventually become that callous leader who does not have time to engage with the people in your organization. Refocus on your values in the day-to-day implementation of your leadership, and you can steer back to your commitment to vision and values.

Like their leader, a group also needs an explicit set of values to anchor decision-making. Without it, people are more vulnerable to being governed by their own biases. You may be easily swayed by the person with the loudest voice, the person with the slickest presentation, or the person who speaks first. Without articulated principles, you can create a chaotic culture, in which people feel like they have to jockey hard and act fast to get their way, instead of a culture in which people believe their voices will be heard and will feel comfortable taking the time to hear everyone. It's important for your people to know that their concerns will be considered earnestly—this has an important impact on the culture you are trying to create.

Without explicit values, you might flip-flop on your guiding principles. When people are confronted with moral dilemmas, the solution comes quickly and intuitively, not deliberately and analytically. The deliberate analysis comes later, when we need to justify those intuitive decisions (Haidt, 2001). This could lead you to feeling confident in your decision, even when it is not rooted in your values.

We made sure our departmental practices were consistent with our values with the understanding that values—like institutions—must be revisited as we grow. We placed our core values in our Strategic Five-Year Plan so that, when we update our strategic plan, we will revisit our values. Whenever the department wants to, it can again engage in the process of creating a new core values document. If the department has changed in fundamental ways, our values might too.

The stories I have told in this chapter reveal the luxury of leading in academia. The primary task of an academic leader is to understand the goals of those we are leading and then support their efforts toward these goals. The principles of collegial governance, academic freedom, and freedom of expression are bedrock principles that distinguish universities from businesses. A university differs from a business not just in its mission but in its governance: a department chair is not a middle manager who directs the activities of the department's members (faculty, staff, and students) and who is directed in turn by more senior managers. Department chairs are agents in the governance of the organization. For this reason, leadership in an academic setting can be meaningful, rewarding, and radically inclusive.

I was lucky to have weekly conversations with Gail, who reminded me again and again that leadership is not about control, but about clarity, purpose, and courage. Leadership is listening, not making decisions in a silo. Consensus is not always easy—but it is fair, inclusive, and creative. And in a world that too often favors speed over reflection, it offers something radical: the time and space to listen.

Following a values-based approach, we made measurable progress in reintegrating members into our community, rebuilding trust, and fostering a culture of calm, collaboration, and care. Grounded in shared values, our department was no longer reacting to the crisis but instead moving intentionally toward a shared vision. I look forward to seeing whether these values and processes will continue to influence the department's culture after I am chair.

I'll admit that I wanted my supervisors to notice my impactful work. Given a complex task and little support from above, I thought I was knocking it out of the park. Little did I know that while the department started on the path to healing, my challenges as an individual were just beginning. I didn't know people would be required to bring a "support person" to meetings with me—because I would be deemed unsafe to meet with. I didn't know that I would be banned from contacting the very DEI office whose support I depended on. I had been given a Glass Cliff leadership opportunity, and I was walking directly toward the cliff.

References

Haidt, J. (2001). The emotional dog and its rational tail: A social intuitionist approach to moral judgment. *Psychological Review, 108*, 814–834. https://doi.org/10.1037/ 0033-295X.108.4.814

Schwartz, S. H. (2012). An overview of the Schwartz theory of basic values. *Online Readings in Psychology and Culture, 2*(1), 11. https://doi.org/10.9707/2307- 0919.1116

5

The Glass Cliff

Kim Campbell became leader of Canada's Progressive Conservative Party in June 1993, following the resignation of Prime Minister Brian Mulroney. Mulroney had led the party since 1983 and served as prime minister from 1984 to 1993, but his popularity had sharply declined. Campbell succeeded Mulroney and was sworn in as Canada's first—and to date, only—female prime minister. Her tenure lasted just over four months, at which point the Progressive Conservatives suffered the worst defeat of any governing party in Canadian history. Campbell lost her seat.

The term "Glass Cliff" was coined in 2005 to describe the finding that women are overrepresented in precarious leadership positions (Ryan & Haslam, 2005). When an organization is in crisis and the risk of failure is high, it is more likely that a woman or a member of a minority group will be promoted to leadership roles. A recent analysis revealed that companies that appointed women to the board were more likely to have had poor performance in the previous five months compared to companies that appointed men to the board. Within Fortune 500 companies, those with weak performance are more likely to promote women, compared to companies with strong performance (Cook & Glass, 2014). High-risk legal cases are more likely to be assigned to female lawyers compared to cases that are likely winnable (Ashby et al., 2006). Female politicians are more likely to be put up for candidacy for seats that are hard to win (Ryan et al., 2010). In college sports, Black coaches are more likely to be promoted into leadership following a losing streak (Cook & Glass, 2013).

Accepting such a precarious leadership opportunity has an impact on the evaluation of this new leader's performance. Glass Cliff leaders are subjected to greater scrutiny than their white, male counterparts (Cook & Glass, 2013). The tenure of Glass Cliff leaders is shorter compared to leaders in organizations that are not in crisis (McCullough, 2014). The Glass Cliff leader's reputation is at stake, as they will be associated with the crisis even if they were not in leadership when the crisis began.

One explanation for the Glass Cliff phenomenon is that women and BIPOC leaders think that this leadership opportunity may be the only one they will ever be offered (McCullough, 2014). It may be the only leadership opportunity that they've ever been offered. A cisgender white man might anticipate that on his upward trajectory there will be more appealing leadership opportunities. For him, taking on a complex leadership role that seems both difficult and likely to fail is unattractive and unnecessary.

There haven't been the same kind of statistical analyses showing that transgender people experience Glass Cliff leadership, but it stands to reason that the phenomenon might be similar. Before my department was in crisis, I was never considered for the position of chair. I was stepping into a situation that others had declined. The job was seen as challenging, maybe even impossible. I accepted it believing I could help people. What I didn't yet understand was how deeply the dynamics of the Glass Cliff would shape my tenure.

When organizations are already in trouble, that's when they're most likely to bring in a woman, a person of color, or a marginalized person to lead the distressed organization. Although I didn't understand it when I took the job, my workplace challenges were disturbingly predictable. It wasn't a real opportunity. It was a rescue mission, and the boat was already sinking.

Clarity Was My Responsibility

It was never a possibility that I would not send a back-to-school email to my department during this time of crisis and confusion. When our department was searching for a chair, a "summary of opportunities" was circulated by the dean's office, saying "The Chair will need to help address the current situation and assist in restoring open and trustful communication between faculty, departmental staff, graduate students, and the University Administration." I had assumed that obligation.

I spent over two weeks developing an email designed to address our students' request for more information and to update our confused community. I contacted the students who had written an open letter to the president asking for information. I asked them what they needed, and I shared drafts of my email with them. I contacted students who were members of our department's student DEI group and asked them for feedback on drafts. I spoke to people who had been personally impacted by the well-publicized claims of sexual assault and harassment and asked for their feedback. I revised my back-to-school email in response to every bit of feedback.

The university had hired a "workplace restoration" consultant to work with our department and another consultant specializing in communications. I worked with the communications specialist to make sure we were on the same page about what was to be communicated in the email, and she sent me a draft. After I had spent weeks talking to people across the department and I thought I had a good handle on what people were thinking and how people wanted to move forward, I reached out to the restoration consultant. I didn't want to leave any stone unturned. I asked if she had heard any perspectives that I hadn't heard. She said she had not, but she encouraged me to continue to "Get curious and listen to your students," advice that I kept in mind throughout my term.

Ordinarily, the timing of my email would be up to me, but the circumstances were not ordinary. I was confronted with a deadline when a reporter from the local newspaper contacted me and demanded to know how students could feel safe in my department. At first the request was polite: "With all the attention on the department last year for allegations of misconduct involving professors, we would like to share your perspective on how the department plans to move forward and keep students safe and protected this year." She asked me for an interview.

An interview with the media regarding the recent debacle was unthinkable. I had not been given any media training, and the university had neither shared all of the reports from their investigations nor advised me on what I could share with the media. I had not been prepped for it. I wanted to hand this media communication over to the university and hide under a rock, but in the final days of August, the university's spokesperson was on vacation.

On August 30th, I reached out to the manager of communications employed by our Faculty of Science. I asked, "Do you have a quick response for reporters who want to know how we are going to keep the students safe? They want a response before the first day of class. They would prefer to set up an interview." He told me that the chief executive of Internal and External Engagement was on vacation and would not be back until September 7th, well after the first day of class. He added, "Not sure who's the primary spokesperson."

After I had ignored the media request for several days, the reporter emailed, "I am hoping to hear from you by 5 p.m. tomorrow. If we do not hear from you, we will unfortunately have to write that you did not respond to our request." I surmised that such a statement would not be good—for the university, for my department, or for me. Instead of giving this reporter an interview—the very idea terrified me—I finalized the email I had been working on. And then I sent the email that would prove to be a Rorschach test.

Dear Members of our Community,

A new school year is about to launch, and many of us are feeling that back-to-school excitement. I would like to thank all of you for making it through the past year. I can't tell you how grateful I am to all of you who were able to listen to each other, learn about our community, and re-commit to our core value of continuous improvement.

As a newly appointed chair, I am committed to working together to foster a learning and working environment that is safe for all students, staff, and faculty. I have been asked by a number of people, including undergraduate students, graduate students, and reporters, how students are going to feel safe in our department when classes resume this fall, following the recent investigations of discrimination, harassment and sexual violence that involved several department members. This email is my response.

First, let me be very clear that it is my intention to ensure that our department is an environment where sexual violence, discrimination, and harassment are not tolerated. Reports of sexually inappropriate behaviour will be taken seriously. Anyone who comes forward with a complaint of sexual violence, discrimination, or harassment should be met with compassion, listened to earnestly, and provided with accurate information about their options. I understand the gravity of this obligation in the context of a world where, historically, complainants have not always been taken seriously.

Second, I want to be clear that although you read in the Daily News that some faculty members were suspended, no faculty member was, in fact, "suspended." The term "suspension" implies guilt and a consequent disciplinary action, and this language should not have been used. In fact, some individuals were placed on non-disciplinary administrative leaves. These leaves were initiated prior to any investigation, were without prejudice, and did not imply guilt. Critically, according to policy, they were not punishments. Instead, these administrative leaves were meant to ensure the integrity of the investigations. The University Administration hired an outside independent investigator. Investigations involved multiple interviews with complainants and respondents as well as a review of much additional evidence.

Although the first respondent is still to be tried in court, all other respondents were found not to have violated *any* University policies, including the sexual violence policy, the discrimination and harassment policy, and the faculty code of conduct (which requires ethical and professional behavior). As a result of these investigations, non-disciplinary administrative leaves were ended.

Third, you would have read in the Daily News that the department has a "degree of complacency that has let inappropriate behaviours go unchecked." Let me be clear: The department leadership will not be complacent if harm is inflicted on our students. If a complaint of assault or harassment were to come to the attention of the leadership of our department, the appropriate response, per policy, would be to pass that complaint onto an intake office on campus, such as the Sexual Violence Office, which is housed in the DEI Office. This is the action that has been taken in all such cases that have been brought to the attention of department leadership over at least the past decade. Following this referral, the department plays no part in investigations or sanctions, and the relevant University policies do not require that the department be informed of outcomes or even informed when the investigation is complete.

Recent events have highlighted a number of weaknesses in the sexual violence policy and the discrimination and harassment policy, and you can be sure that members of the department will advocate for policy changes that support the safety of all. Complainants of sexual violence and sexual harassment **must** be supported by the University's policies and procedures.

Of course, your feeling of safety will also depend on all of our actions going forward. Faculty members are recommitting to our value of continuous improvement. We are listening to you, and we are learning from you. We are actively working with all stakeholders to develop action plans to help us move forward. This message is one such action. We are continuing to work on strengthening best practices through various initiatives including evidence-based training. We will continue to communicate.

This email was difficult to craft. My intention is to share information with you, and I have tried to describe events without commentary. Many people worked with me to craft this email in order to reduce the chances of harm, and I want to thank the students, staff and faculty who helped to check my tone and language.

Together we are moving forward. If you have any concerns, my door is open.

On to a better year,
Mel Rutherford

Late in the week before classes started, I sent my email to our department's faculty, staff, graduate students, and undergraduate students, about 1500 people in all. Knowing that the local media had been hounding me for a message, The Supervisor asked me to send my message to the reporter. "Sorry for the swirling confusion around your contact with the media," she said. "I understand that you issued your welcome back memo to the Department yesterday so perhaps you could share that with the media." I forwarded the email to the reporter. Within the hour, The Supervisor emailed again to tell me that she had changed her mind.

Up to that point, I thought we were collaborating to coordinate an extremely challenging communication, so it was a gut punch when The Supervisor threatened to bring me up on charges under the Faculty Code of Conduct for sending my email to my department.

Denunciation

The following day, I received an email from The Supervisor. "I would like to meet with you and discuss some concerns I have with both the tone and content of the email you sent to the Department." That was my first clue that my term as chair was going to be even more difficult than anticipated.

The Zoom call blinked to life with a chime. On my screen, The Supervisor appeared, framed by the tidy bookshelves of her home office. I sat alone in mine, in what had become my daily uniform during remote work: a crisp collared shirt above the camera line, flannel pajama pants and slippers below. Kahlo, my faithful dachshund, was curled at my feet, unaware that my career was about to lurch sideways.

Although we had known each other for years, The Supervisor told me that we were "virtual strangers" and that "we don't know much about each other." The Supervisor's language—"virtual strangers"—was a signal. She wanted to distance herself from me not just publicly, but personally. Trust had been quietly withdrawn.

The Supervisor wanted to distance herself from my email. She implied that I was playing favorites and taking sides among people in my department when she said, "a department needs a leader that takes everyone's voices into account."

I felt my pulse quicken. She didn't ask me about the weeks of conversations I had had in order to prepare the 777-word email, carefully, transparently, and in consultation with dozens of students, staff, faculty, and her own communications consultant. It had been my first major communication since I took over as chair. I was confident that the message I wrote, marking the beginning of the new September term and a chance at a different future, was calm and compassionate. Responding to the urgent needs of the department, it was, I thought, a model of ethical leadership.

I tried to explain the process—how I'd consulted widely, how students had asked for information, how I followed the communication goals my predecessor had developed, how the reporter had pressured me for comment, and how the university's own silence had left me with little information. She wasn't there to listen.

She said, "I first want to just ask you if you think your role is to ensure that all members have a space at the table?" I told her that yes, "I think that one of the most exciting parts about this email was the process. I was hearing so many different perspectives." "I talked to so many different students. I talked to students I hadn't ever met before." I told her, "I was reaching out to places where I could hear perspectives." Given my commitment to compassion and the care I took in listening to what people needed, it was puzzling that my message could be interpreted as harmful. I told her that I was proud of my email and proud of the process that I had followed to create the email. That really didn't seem to be what she was looking for.

She instructed me to send a follow-up email and told me, "I want it to clearly state that I hadn't been involved in the email, didn't approve it, didn't know about it," each syllable sharp and clipped. Something in me sank.

This rebuke was shocking and stressful and new. This was the first time in my life I had been reprimanded by a supervisor. I've always been the good student, the productive colleague, and now the trusted leader. My 16-year-old son, overhearing the conversation from the next room, was stunned: "Who was that?" he asked. "My boss," I replied. It was already clear that my leadership would be judged through a different, more unforgiving lens. What I knew for sure, sitting in that small room with the dog curled at my feet and the biggest microphone I had ever owned was this: I had acted with integrity and led with compassion. I had done my job.

Like The Supervisor, my university also seemed to be susceptible to the idea that I was harming students. My appointment as the first transgender department chair had been announced in the local newspaper, so the university's reputation benefited from my appointment, since they appeared to be supportive of trans leadership. This publicity would make me vulnerable to public criticism nine weeks later when my university publicly disavowed me in the same newspaper.

They distanced themselves from my email and publicly denounced me. The university was quoted as saying, "The message (from Rutherford) is not aligned with the university's values or its commitment to working with survivors and consulting and engaging people across the department to build an inclusive and safe environment for everyone within the department." They hadn't asked me a single question about the process behind the email. Not one. They never asked who I consulted, how many hours I spent talking to people, or how carefully I listened.

Eventually, The Supervisor decided that she, herself, would send a follow-up message to my department. She wrote to my entire department, "On August 31 you received an email from the Chair of the Department. While I was not aware of the email in advance and do not endorse the content, I have since been made aware of the negative impacts the email has had on some members of the department. Through this message, I want to reaffirm my commitment to creating and promoting a more inclusive experience for everyone."

That was it. No specific concerns were named. Her "more inclusive" wording implied that my message was somehow less inclusive. Her reference to "negative impacts" clearly suggests that I was somehow harming "some members" of my department. I was so new to the role that I was still in the process of building trust among the people I was leading, so her communication to my department was a threat to my success as a leader. The vague accusation that I had harmed people echoed loudly against the backdrop of anti-trans tropes that paint transgender people as dangerous, unstable, or, most perniciously, harmful to students.

When I initially sent out my email, I got dozens of emails thanking me for clarifying the situation. Students thanked me for communicating directly and compassionately with them. One person told me my compassion brought a tear to her eye. Colleagues told me that we were opening the door for compassionate and frank conversation. After The Supervisor's note went out and more emails arrived—this time expressing confusion that she wasn't supporting me.

Am I the Problem?

Had I done something wrong? How was my message so misunderstood by The Supervisor? Why didn't she trust that I was acting in the best interest of my department? I was striving for transparency and compassion. I worked with students, staff, and faculty to ensure the tone was careful and informative. I explicitly affirmed our department's commitment to safety and explained the university's procedures. And yet, this communication became the basis for suspicion. While I was trying to rebuild a fractured department—fostering healing, supporting colleagues, and refocusing on our collective mission—I was being publicly denounced.

When I became chair, Gail asked me a series of questions designed to set me up for success. One question was: "How might you be your own worst enemy?" Easy question. I replied, "I can be very quiet. There are a variety of ways that people interpret my silence. Sometimes my silence hinders relationship building." I found building a constructive relationship with The Supervisor impossible, and I know that part of that was because I am quiet. I rarely spoke up and never talked back. Could I have done something different?

Decades earlier, when I was a graduate student, I was working as a teaching assistant for my supervisor, Leda Cosmides. Leda is very smart and very diligent. I rarely saw her make mistakes. But one day, I was grading a midterm exam and noticed that most students got one of the questions "wrong." I looked at the answer key and realized that it was the answer key that was wrong. I called Leda.

"The answer key says C is the correct answer, but it should be A." Leda said, "No, the answer is C." It was a question about a tricky concept, and the question required you to step back from your intuition. It was the kind of question that you would expect someone else to get confused about, which made it easy for her to dismiss my suggestion. We went several rounds of "No, I'm right," "No, you're wrong," and we were both completely confident in our beliefs.

I took a risk. I knew she trusted me, I knew she thought I was smart, and I had faith that I could test our relationship a little bit. I said, "Leda, I need you to listen to me. You are not seeing this the right way. Please take a moment to think about this." That stopped her. She took a moment and reevaluated her answer. She took that moment because I spoke up and because she trusted me. The answer was A.

I've thought many times about whether I could have similarly caused The Supervisor to reexamine her deeply held beliefs. I imagine how things might be different if I had said, "Please stop for a second and listen to me. I need you to trust me. You have misunderstood this entire situation." What if she, like Leda, had taken a beat and trusted me enough to wonder if I was saying something important?

I didn't ever speak to The Supervisor that directly. I didn't have faith in our relationship. She was my boss. She was curt and stern. I was intimidated by her. If I had it all to do again, would I have the courage to speak up, to interrupt her entrenched perspective? I'd like to imagine that I would, but I doubt it.

A year and a half into my term, we had worked through the grievances that members of my department had filed against the university's administration, and I was hopeful that The Supervisor and I could move forward, with a relationship that was at least professional if not friendly. After our tense meeting to discuss my back-to-school email, I had sent her an email asking her for a fresh start on our relationship. I thought we could develop enough trust to have a workable relationship. I was not expecting to see her tallest finger standing alone.

We were in a one-on-one meeting, just the two of us in her office. She required me to meet with her monthly in order to report on activities in my department, so I had become familiar with the view of tree branches outside the window, and with the rigid wooden chair I sat in at the round table in her office. On the table between us sat a summary of the Inquiry and Remedy Committee's findings, information that I had shared with Michelle Flaherty for her investigation. The Supervisor's middle finger, standing like an exclamation mark, was accompanied by the usual profanity. As if her feelings toward me could be clarified, she added "I'm tired of you." I understood that our relationship was irreparable.

In the Halls of Power

I was looking forward to my meeting with The Administrator.

I had filed a complaint after my mandatory monthly meeting with The Supervisor had included profanity. I had asked for a new reporting structure so that I could report to a different supervisor. The task fell to one of the university's highest-ranking administrators—I'll call her The Administrator—to make a decision regarding my complaint, and I had received an email from her executive assistant asking, "Would you kindly let me know if you would be available to meet on Monday?"

At breakfast before I headed off to the meeting, Melanie expressed relief. She knew how much stress I was under reporting to The Supervisor. Now she had hope. Someone was finally going to respond to my pleas and set up a new reporting structure. Finally, someone cared—someone who was in a position to keep me safe at work. We both wondered what solutions she would come up with to ensure that I could have the protection I needed to do my best work as department chair. Was I going to get a new boss? Perhaps my excruciating meetings with The Supervisor were over. In any case, I was expecting the meeting to be a follow-up to my complaint.

When I arrived, one of the highest-ranking members of the university's human resources office—I'll call her Human Resources—was already seated at the grand, rectangular table. We met in an interior room of The Administrator's office suite. The office is grand and imposing. Like the building itself, the interior of the office is stone, and it has a stately stone fireplace. It was the kind of room designed to remind you of the institution's power.

The Administrator, a blonde, cherubic woman who was younger than one might anticipate given her position, sat at the head of her table which was crafted out of carved wood. The meeting started friendly. I told her that my sons swim competitively in the university pool. The Administrator is an engineer, and I told her that over the weekend I had seen the dean of engineering deliver opening remarks at a huge robotics competition that had taken place in the same building as my sons' swim meet. She seemed to be on the same page, as she shared that those competitions were exciting, community-building events in the faculty of engineering. She was trying to get me to relax and to trust her. I felt like the meeting was going well.

I went on to tell The Administrator, quite excitedly, about the great progress we had made in the department over the past two years. I told her that in order to tackle the challenge of guiding our distressed department, I had adopted a values-based approach to governance, prioritizing integrity and compassion. I told her about the core values exercise and the fact that we had incorporated the viewpoints of faculty, staff, postdocs, graduate students, and undergraduate students. I shared how pleased I was that we had built undergraduate input into the process. I told her that we had used our values as a foundation to build a mission and vision statement as well as our strategic five-year plan.

It was refreshing being able to talk about my accomplishments, given my difficult relationship with The Supervisor. Having this opportunity to tell one of the highest leaders in the university about this work was satisfying. I had heard that she was looking for faculty members that she could mentor into greater leadership positions. She was particularly interested in developing and mentoring women, and she had taken a good friend of mine out to a one-on-one mentorship lunch. I was hoping that she would be impressed by my ability to lead my department through a crisis. Maybe she would pick me for mentorship. I was hopeful that we were at least creating a new relationship between my department and the upper administration. It was only in retrospect that I realized that The Administrator and Human Resources were not reflecting my enthusiasm.

The tone of the meeting shifted suddenly when she asked me "Do you regret agreeing to be chair of the department?" Wait, what? It was a question weighted with implication. What trap had I walked into? I had been invited into this office of highest power, unaware of the danger. I had not thought to bring a witness. Or an emotional support person. Or a lawyer. Suddenly the meeting was a lot less fun. I could hear my pulse, and I knew that I must be turning red. The word-for-word notes that I was taking became harder to decipher as my hand became unsteady. The hope that Melanie had expressed over breakfast evaporated. The camaraderie I had felt over the joy of robotics competitions was never there.

I responded firmly, describing how proud I was of our accomplishments and how deeply I believed in leading with integrity and compassion. I told her that I did not regret accepting the role of chair. I told her that in fact, the work I was doing in the department, although challenging, was meaningful and fulfilling. She shared a message she had received about me the previous day. A faculty member from another department within the university wanted me to be replaced as chair. She said, "I am shocked by Mel's behavior. I had no idea he would ally himself with that cohort. Before being chair, he was largely ignored. He was left to work alone. He didn't rock the boat."

She asked me if I was surprised. I was a little surprised that someone would reach out to The Administrator. If someone had questions about my leadership, why not talk to me? But I wasn't surprised by the content of the message; I was familiar with transphobia. It was clear that The Administrator was persuaded by this message. Not only did the upper administration have no strategy for reintegrating the accused into my department, they were not willing to stand by me while I did this work. The Administrator offered me a year's leave and relief from my teaching assignments if I resigned as chair.

The Administrator then made the extraordinary claim that our department's strategic plan—the one that I had just excitedly told her about — had been developed in secret. She said that I had not told The Supervisor that we were engaging in a planning process and that I had "circumvented her input."

The fact that our department was engaged in strategic planning was known both to the public and to The Supervisor. When I was interviewed for the position of chair, I was asked how I would approach creating a strategic plan. Half a year into my term, I was interviewed for the Faculty of Science newsletter, and I told the Manager of Communications that we were about to start strategic planning, in response to his "What's the one thing you hope to accomplish as Chair?" question. I suppose The Administrator didn't have time to read the Faculty of Science newsletter.

I explained to The Administrator that I had sent a letter to The Supervisor prior to developing our strategic planning, stating "We have begun our Strategic Planning exercise which will culminate in a 5-year plan." I told her about the process: "We have hired a consultant to help guide us through a core values exercise, and she is meeting with faculty, staff, postdocs, graduate students, and undergraduate students so that our community's values can serve as a foundation for our planning." I even asked her for money: "We have one-time need to complete our core value exercise ($10,000) and our Strategic Planning ($10,000)."

When I told The Administrator about this letter, she said, "That is not the information I have." She appeared more comfortable to be left with her belief that I had circumvented input. Juxtaposing my claim that I had communicated about our strategic planning both to The Supervisor and the public with The Administrator's belief that we had created the plan in secret, she came to believe that I was being deceitful, one of the most enduring and socially acceptable anti-trans stereotypes.

The Administrator told me our strategic plan was "not inclusive of women." I could feel the weight of the accusation—implied was that I, as chair and a transgender man, had failed women in the department. She said our strategic plan failed to "advance the principles of equity, diversity, and inclusion," and it ran "counter to the institutional priority of advancing inclusive excellence." She said that the plan did not "recognize Indigenous ways of being, knowing and doing." She told me that our strategic plan "amplifies a small number of voices." I listened carefully, silently recalling the months of dedicated work—faculty retreats, student roundtables, and collaborative drafting sessions, all conducted by a large and representative committee—that had brought our plan to life. None of that seemed to matter. The Administrator was not curious about the processes we had followed in our strategic planning.

This was not a narrative I had ever faced. When I told later friends that the Administrator said I didn't listen to women's voices, reactions ranged from amused to bewildered. Most of the closest people in my life are women. My book club consists of nine women and me. I think of myself as good at responding to constructive feedback, but this feedback was outlandish and unactionable. I couldn't figure out what the Administrator was talking about.

Regarding the complaint I had filed, I would not be getting the new reporting structure I had asked for. The Administrator told me that she supports The Supervisor "100%." Her decision was that a "single incident involving inappropriate language does not always constitute a violation of the Human Rights Code."

I had not mentioned the Human Rights Code. I had asked for a new supervisory structure. "You are not to circumvent or avoid communication with [The Supervisor]."

I came to understand that the purpose of this meeting was neither to celebrate our department's progress nor to make my workplace safer. I came to suspect that Human Resources had been brought in to document the meetings and develop a dossier of evidence that might be used to remove me from my role. The Administrator told me, "Maybe your stepping down would be a good idea." Human Resources said they could identify someone to step in as chair. The Administrator told me that the university's priority is equity and inclusion and that that was not the culture in my department. The meeting ended with The Administrator telling me that it was urgent that I be replaced as chair because the administration "wants to create a department where people feel welcome and there is equity."

Her follow-up letter read, "you stated that you advised [The Supervisor] of the strategic plan in January 2022," and "This is not consistent with my understanding." I never understood why she didn't just ask for the letter, since I had it and The Supervisor had it. She also said that our strategic plan "is counter to the institutional priority of advancing inclusive excellence," again without showing any curiosity about the ten-month process we used to create the strategic plan. She didn't mince words: "I noted in our meeting that the status quo could not continue. Your approach does not advance the principles of equity, diversity, and inclusion or recognize Indigenous Ways of Being, Knowing and Doing."

I needed help. I was succeeding at leading my department, but I was completely failing at managing up. The juxtaposition was stark and scary.

Unanimous Support

Prior to this meeting with The Administrator, I really thought I was knocking it out of the park. For two years, I had been connecting with people, I had been doing good work, and I had felt energized by leading my department back to work. I had a plan, I had my values to guide me, and I could tell that I was making progress. Faculty, staff, and students frequently told me how much they appreciated my leadership. People went out of their way to thank Melanie for allowing me to serve the department when they saw her.

I had been intentional and deliberate in planning the inclusive processes that had created our strategic plan. I was confused by her ire. As one of the most powerful people at the university, I wondered what she might do to harm me. I was tenured, so it seemed unlikely that I would lose my job. Would she remove me from my role as chair? Would she ruin my reputation, telling others that I am not inclusive of women, or that I don't recognize Indigenous ways of being, knowing, and doing? It seemed clear that any bridge to higher-ranking leadership positions had collapsed. Did I need to be planning a move to another university, or to another career? After this gut punch, my confidence and my energy began to wane. I felt deflated.

I left that meeting facing the half kilometer walk back to my department and my colleagues. I didn't even make it to the sidewalk before I phoned Melanie and told her I was going to have to resign. Then I called my predecessor. He listened to my story empathetically. He told me that sometimes administrators see if you will step aside without a fight. He told me that I didn't have to resign.

With The Administrator's attempt to remove me as chair, I realized that I needed to hear from my department, to find out how my efforts had been perceived. I went back to my department and told our associate chairs about my meeting with The Administrator. They were horrified and offered to support me. One of them organized a meeting of all of our faculty members (minus me) to discuss whether they wanted me to continue as chair. They all did.

This associate chair and our department manager then created an anonymous survey. Although the people who had attended the meeting were unanimous in their support, it was possible that a dissenter would not want to speak up in a meeting. An anonymous survey might allow an opportunity for criticism. In fact, 100% of faculty and staff answered yes to the questions "do you support the work that Mel Rutherford has done as chair," "do you support Mel Rutherford continuing as chair," and "do you feel the department is an inclusive community?" This support from my departmental colleagues was really meaningful to me and gave me tremendous confidence to continue serving as chair. I appreciated their support.

Early in my term as chair, the university had commissioned a third party to take an "Engagement Survey" of people's experience in the workplace. These data were collected from people in my department as well as from departments across campus. My department's scores were consistently above average in response to questions about whether they have an "accessible chair," whether their "chair is approachable," whether they are "treated with respect" by the person they report to, whether the department "supports diversity," and whether they can "bring their whole selves to work." Because my department wanted me to continue to be chair, I made sure The Administrator had both of these datasets.

I might have guessed from our previous meeting, but The Administrator wasn't interested in the data that suggested I was succeeding in leadership. Her legal team wrote, the "University's Engagement Survey was outdated and had uneven response rates." In fact, the data had been collected while I was chair, so it wasn't out of date for our purposes. Her legal team also dismissed the opinions of people who were in my department, saying "Dr. Rutherford created one of those surveys." Actually, I had recused myself from the design and the data collection. I am a scientist, after all. The Administrator must have been frustrated that no one in my department wanted me to step down as chair, but she was determined. She wrote, "I remain concerned that your leadership to date has fostered an environment in which those voices [people who want a change in leadership] cannot be heard, as they do not feel safe." She must have imagined that I was a powerful despot, to silence an entire department.

I was not prepared to give up my calling and let them displace me. Despite The Administrator's offer of an administrative leave, I wrote to The Administrator and Human Resources on April 10, 2023, and told them that I would continue as chair.

> I'm not going to be stepping down from my role as chair right now. We are still in a situation where no one else is eager to hold the position of chair, and I have not yet heard any voices that want a change in leadership at this time. Indeed, I have heard a number of voices in my department who do not think this is a good time for a change in leadership. Furthermore, I have heard very clearly that my colleagues do not want another escalation. They want to "turn down the temperature." That said, I will continue to listen for people who want to chair the department, as well as for voices that are ready for a change in leadership.
>
> As I told you in our meeting, when I became chair, I prioritized the values of integrity and compassion. Our department is in a better place now than it was two years ago, but this continues to be a group that will benefit from compassion and care. For now, I will honor my commitment to them.

Trans Tropes

The Administrator's words were reminiscent of the anti-trans trope that trans men can't be feminist. The idea is that anyone who has transitioned to live as a man has rejected womanhood and, therefore, does not value it. This trope creates an artificial divide between feminists and transgender activists. Dividing feminists from transgender activists is a costly fragmentation of political power, and in the era of Trump, this trope is getting new energy. Although I have spent my adulthood in progressive and activist spaces, I was being accused of not being inclusive of women. I would not have been so accused had I not transitioned.

One age-old anti-trans trope is that transgender people hurt young people. The narrative is not new, but it has taken on new forms in recent years, often by exploiting public fears about child safety. From the claim that drag queen story hours are "grooming" events to the organized efforts of groups like Moms for Liberty who oppose gender-inclusive school policies, the association of trans folks with harm to children has become a political weapon. Florida Governor Ron DeSantis's press secretary tweeted that if you don't support the "Don't say gay" law, "you are probably a groomer or at least you don't denounce the grooming of 4–8 year old children." In March and April of 2022, Fox news commentators began describing parents allowing their children to express transgender identities as "grooming." These campaigns try to claim the moral high ground in the name of their organization: The "Save the Children" campaign sounds so obviously good that it is hard to mount an argument against it.

The Trump administration has amplified anti-trans tropes. Trump has been quite obvious about exploiting the trope that trans people are a threat to women. He announced in his second inaugural address that henceforth "It is the policy of the United States to recognize two sexes, male and female." That same week, he signed Executive Order 14,168, which goes on to read that "These sexes are not changeable and are grounded in fundamental and incontrovertible reality." It is important to understand that this executive order is titled "Defending Women from Gender Ideology Extremism and Restoring Biological Truth to the Federal Government." He wants you to believe that he is defending women. The new administration claims this move will defend women's rights. Linking trans erasure to women's safety is an attempt to make transphobia not only socially acceptable, but imperative.

The Trump administration has made it a priority to create barriers to participation in athletics, to participation in the military, and to medical care. The ferocity of the anti-trans campaign juxtaposed with the number of transgender people in the population has confused some people. When Utah's Governor Cox vetoed a bill banning trans participation in sports, he pointed out, "75,000 high school kids participating in high school sports in Utah. 4 transgender kids playing high school sports in Utah. 1 transgender student playing girls sports" (Cox, 2022).

Kush Desai, the white house deputy press secretary, was asked why anti-trans policies had become such a priority. He replied, "The American people voiced a resounding Election Day mandate to restore common sense and reject the radical ideology that paved the way for irreversible child mutilation procedures and the undermining of girls' sports by biological men across our country. The Trump administration is committed to delivering on this mandate" (Christensen, 2025).

Anti-trans caricatures, though not named directly, saturated how I was perceived and undermined my work from the inside. I wanted to continue, and I was determined to lead. I chose to persevere. I resisted the narrative that framed me as the problem and instead focused on the work ahead, reaffirming my commitment to serve with integrity, compassion, and transparency. I had been called, and, if necessary, I would lead without the support of the administration.

The Administrator was not done with me.

References

Ashby, J. S., Ryan, M. K., & Haslam, S. A. (2006). Legal work and the glass cliff: Evidence that women are preferentially selected to lead problematic cases. *William & Mary Journal of Women and the Law, 13,* 775. https://scholarship.law.wm.edu/wmjowl/vol13/iss3/5

Christensen, J. (2025). Trump administration takes all-of-government approach to target transgender community. https://www.cnn.com/2025/07/21/health/trans-community-trump-all-of-government

Cook, A., & Glass, C. (2013). Glass cliffs and organizational saviors: Barriers to minority leadership in work organizations? *Social Problems, 60*(2), 168–187. https://doi.org/10.1525/sp.2.13.60.2.168

Cook, A., & Glass, C. (2014). Above the glass ceiling: When are women and racial/ethnic minorities promoted to CEO? *Strategic Management Journal, 35*(7), 1080–1089. https://doi.org/10.1002/smj.2161

Cox, S.J. (2022). Why I'm vetoing HB11. https://governor.utah.gov/press/gov-cox-why-im-vetoing-hb11/

McCullough, DG. (2014, August 8). Women CEOs: Why companies in crisis hire minorities—And then fire them. *The Guardian.* https://www.theguardian.com/sustainable-business/2014/aug/05/fortune-500-companies-crisis-woman-ceo-yahoo-xerox-jc-penny-economy.

Ryan, M. K., & Haslam, S. A. (2005). The glass cliff: Evidence that women are over-represented in precarious leadership positions. *British Journal of Management, 16*(2), 81–90. https://doi.org/10.1111/j.1467-8551.2005.00433.x

Ryan, M. K., Haslam, S. A., & Kulich, C. (2010). Politics and the glass cliff: Evidence that women are preferentially selected to contest hard-to-win seats. *Psychology of Women Quarterly, 34*(1), 56–64. https://doi.org/10.1111/j.1471-6402.2009.01541.x

6

A Workplace Investigation and a Secret Report

One month after my initial meeting with The Administrator, she called me back for another meeting in her office, this time with a larger group. Human Resources was there again, ready to document the scripted rebuke. The university's Director of Human Rights, a lawyer, attended the meeting. I brought a colleague from my faculty association as a witness, and it felt good to have someone on my side. The ordeal was so bewildering that I needed someone to confirm that it was actually happening.

The Administrator read from prepared notes. It appeared that she was trying to persuade everyone in the room, including me perhaps, that it would be best if I were removed as chair of the department. She offered a series of reasons.

She started, "I do want to continue to highlight some of the ongoing concerns in the department." She mentioned the data I had sent to her from the university-commissioned engagement survey, which strongly suggested that my leadership was above average. "So, I understand the engagement survey was done December 2021 and January 2022. So, that's quite some time ago." We were meeting in May of 2023. She also commented on the response rate, "I also understood that 14 of the 27 faculty only participated, 5 of 10 postdocs, 18 of 24 staff ... ." Adding the word "only" made it sound as if she thought that this response rate was low, although she didn't compare our response rate to that of other departments. I thought we had a pretty good response rate for a survey that just showed up in people's email inbox. She acknowledged the more recent anonymous survey showing unanimous support for my leadership and asked, "How many faculty members did respond, and what considerations went into the design of the survey?" I told her that all of our faculty and all of our staff responded and that responses were anonymous. She moved on.

She tried to suggest that under my leadership our department was not supportive of students' progress. "So, certainly there have been a number of concerns expressed about support and openness with students in this program." I told her that the department was adamant that "every student who's currently enrolled in the program will have our full support until they graduate or leave the program." She quickly challenged, "And you have documentation on that? Because that is very different information than what has been received." I told her that I could give meeting minutes if she needed them and asked for clarification about what her concerns were. She said, "You're aware of what the situation is, Mel." At that point I was pretty sure neither of us understood what she was accusing me of.

I assured her "Everyone in the department knows we're committed to the students who are currently in the program, and that we will see them through graduation." She said, "That's different than the information we have, and I think you've seen that information." I had not. My mind was scrambling to make sense of her accusations. My whole life I had had the support of supervisors. I wanted and expected my supervisors to like me. I didn't have trouble getting along with people. Here we sat in the seat of the university's power, while Human Resources and the Director of Human Rights watched The Administrator accuse me of .... something. It was disheartening. I knew we were well beyond her thanking me for the work I was doing to repair the department.

The Administrator then accused me of financial mismanagement. She said that my department had "submitted a significant graduate deficit budget." Among the many stressors the department had incurred, one was a blow to the budget. In 2020, graduate supervisors had been put on leave while allegations were being investigated. Eleven graduate students had been separated from their supervisors and from the financial support of their supervisors' research grants. Most of these students were also granted extra time to complete their degrees, which increased the cost of their support. The department spent $226,000 supporting these students and had to hire temporary instructors to cover courses. When I stepped into my role, this became my problem. A department that had always been fiscally sound suddenly had a budget deficit, and I was being reprimanded, a classic example of the cost of accepting a Glass Cliff leadership position.

As confusing as these accusations were, The Administrator went on to accuse me of some even less specific failings. She said, "more recently, I've been made aware of a number of administrative concerns." She paused and consulted her notes at length. Although I had the impression that she was well prepped for this meeting, she must not have been able to make sense of her notes because she finally said that my supervisor "will be following up on some of these administrative concerns that have come forward. There are a number of concerns that will be coming forward." The concerns never managed to come forward.

I sat in this old bastion of authority with a group of people who held enough power to unnerve me. I had communicated clearly that I intended to continue as chair, so this exquisitely orchestrated meeting seemed like overkill. I wanted them to leave me alone so that I could continue my work.

Scrutiny

One of the characteristics of a Glass Cliff appointment is scrutiny. The Glass Cliff leader may be associated with a crisis, even when the crisis predates their leadership. I've been criticized and scrutinized both publicly and privately since taking on the task of repairing my department. When I was invited to give a talk in the department of sociology about my experience as our department's first transgender chair, I was surprised to see in the audience two people from the university's human resources department. How often does HR send people to attend academic talks? I smiled and waved and later emailed to thank them for attending.

During my term as chair, I was called into a number of disciplinary meetings as the scrutiny intensified. Two years into my term as department chair, I was growing used to intense scrutiny of my actions, but the emotional cost was growing. I wasn't just navigating unconscious bias. I was being documented as a failed leader. Institutional actors were creating records to support their perceptions of me. I didn't know of other department chairs who were managing this level of scrutiny or this volume of corrective oversight.

I learned that the format of these disciplinary meetings is formulaic. They don't tell you ahead of time that it is going to be a disciplinary meeting so that you don't know to bring a support person. They don't tell you the agenda unless you ask, and I've discovered that they sometimes don't provide an agenda even if you ask. Human Resources is always there, having arrived before the meeting starts. Twice I've been greeted by a lawyer in a meeting I've been required to attend, but I have never been told that I might need a lawyer.

These meetings were paranoia-inducing, leading me to wonder what other people on campus might believe about me. I was aware that The Administrator and The Supervisor discussed me with my colleagues—and not positively. At least some people had heard things that made them step away from me: The Director of Human Rights, who witnessed the second meeting with The Administrator, first disconnected from me on LinkedIn and later blocked me altogether. Maybe she believed that I was failing in leadership. Maybe she believed a relationship with me was dangerous to her own career. How was I to know?

Since enduring these disciplinary meetings, I have spoken to another transgender leader who has a relatively high-ranking administrative position in another university. He shared that earlier in his career, when he had been trying to move into leadership roles, there were colleagues who were resistant to his advancing. It was clear to him that these people were uncomfortable with his gender. They didn't want him to advance, and they really didn't want to work with him at all. I surmised that I would not be subjected to these meetings if I had not transitioned. These meetings were traumatizing, I assume intentionally, and they made it difficult for me to get my job done.

A Workplace Investigation

The Administrator had a couple more tricks up her sleeve. Choosing to remain chair was an act of resistance. It was a commitment to defy stereotypes, to challenge exclusionary narratives, and to embody leadership that embraces complexity, compassion, and integrity. After I affirmed my intention to fulfill my commitment to my department came another unprecedented step: a formal workplace investigation.

The Administrator hired a law firm that conducts workplace investigations. The law firm wrote, "The interviews are anticipated to commence within one (1) week of the University's approval, and we expect to conclude all interviews by July 31, 2023." The plan was to focus on whether people trusted me to foster "inclusion, equity, belonging, psychological health, and safety," which was similar to the focus of both the Engagement Survey that the university had commissioned and the more recent survey my department conducted. The Administrator had agreed to pay the law firm to conduct interviews but would not pay them to do any fact-checking of anything that was asserted in the interviews. "The Report will reflect only the Participants' version of events without further fact-checking on the veracity of such accounts."

The fact that The Administrator was unwilling to accept the evidence that I was succeeding as a leader suggests that it was hard for her to evaluate my effectiveness in my Glass Cliff leadership position. If you were sincerely evaluating someone's leadership, you would not discount the positive material that supported good leadership and then commission negative feedback. There appeared to be a bias against me. The Administrator told me in a letter titled "Leadership in the department—Continued Discussion" that "Once I have reviewed that report [from the Workplace Investigation], I will resume our conversation about your leadership and the best interests of the department."

Four very senior members of my department stepped forward to take the unnamed but extraordinary leadership task of protecting me. These four people, they called themselves "The Gang of Four," were all senior to me. Two of them had served as mentors to me when I had first been hired. One of them chaired the committee that hired me. They were all willing to do what they could to support our department, and they were invested in my success both as a faculty member and as chair of the department. One of these colleagues wrote to me "You shouldn't try to manage this on your own—it's too important to your future and the future of the department. And we want to support you!"

The Gang of Four tried to talk The Administrator out of such an overt attempt to discredit my work. They were firm and direct in their communications with The Administrator, advocating for me and for the department. They wrote to her in a letter stating, "this letter is not marked confidential," that "We were surprised and somewhat disappointed by your May 12, 2023 replies to our letter dated May 7, 2023. In our letter, we described the damage that would occur to the department if [this investigation] were to go ahead unchanged. Your letter, while acknowledging some of the points we made, indicated that the listening exercise would proceed imminently."

They pointed out that The Administrator already had the information about me that she claimed she needed. "If the purpose of the listening exercise is 'to evaluate the status and effectiveness of DEI initiatives in the department' (theme 3) or 'respect in the workspace and academia' (theme 1), we note that there was a Faculty of Science survey on that topic last fall in which PNB fared comparatively well on precisely these types of within-department items. What additional information is sought?" The survey they refer to was the Engagement Survey, showing that the department was inclusive and accessible under my leadership, scoring well above average on such items. Relatedly, they reminded The Administrator that "the anonymous survey of faculty and staff who report to Dr. Rutherford showed unanimous support for his leadership just a few weeks ago."

They told The Administrator that this investigation would be destructive and further erode trust between the department and the upper administration. The Gang of Four spent hours in conversation with The Administrator and they took their time to craft very carefully worded letters. They told me that it was good that they were involved because it would be difficult for any chair to navigate this alone. Ultimately, they were successful, and The Administrator decided not to investigate me.

A Secret Report

During the second meeting in her impressive office, The Administrator had described a secret report that she somehow knew to expect even though it would not exist for two weeks. Like academic programs everywhere, our graduate and undergraduate programs are reviewed every few years. The review is organized by an external "Council on Quality Assurance" and is meant to follow some fairly rigorous processes that allow a department to reflect on the quality of their programs and also discuss with a panel of reviewers their suggestions for improving that quality. Two years into my term as chair, we hosted three reviewers, one from within our university and two from other universities, who were tasked with reviewing our undergraduate programs. Normally, reviewers submit a report that is available for the department leadership as well as the dean and other administrators to read. In very unusual situations, I was surprised to learn, reviewers could also submit a secret report. In the case of our department, the secret report recommended that I be replaced as chair.

The Administrator described the report with a tone that suggested that she expected her assessment of me to be confirmed, allowing her to remove me from office. She told me, "I understand that the reviewers have identified substantial concerns about your leadership." She said, "this report is pending. But you know, I'm giving you a heads up." Her follow-up letter to the meeting reiterated, "While a report is still pending, I shared with you my understanding that the reviewers identified substantial concerns about your leadership." Fifteen days later, the university received the secret report that The Administrator had somehow foreseen.

On the morning of June 14, 2023, I had the "Summary of Key Points" by 10 o'clock. I opened the properties of the word document and saw that the person listed as the author of the document was Human Resources, the same person who had sat in on my meetings with The Administrator. Human Resources is not normally involved in an academic review. It appeared as if some of these processes were not, in fact, academic in nature.

I was to be shown the entire secret report in The Supervisor's office. I brought two witnesses with me. She tried to dissuade me from bringing witnesses: "There was a confidential report that accompanied the broader one and we would like to discuss that with you. It does contain some sensitive information related to your role as chair so you might want to consider if you want [your two colleagues] to step out for that portion of the conversation." I definitely wanted my colleagues there with me.

The meeting felt stilted and formal, and The Supervisor displayed the entire secret report on the big screen in her office. One comment said "The department Chair did not show up as a leader. He did not appear engaged." I admit that I am a quiet leader. I am a quiet person. But I don't think that there is only one successful way to lead. Our department was well prepared for the review, and I did not need the limelight. I was investing in the leadership development of our associate chair of undergraduate studies, and she had done a fantastic job preparing for the review. I wanted her to shine.

The secret report was critical of our department's consensus-based decision-making. I had shared with our reviewers my recently published article from "The Conversation," describing our department's use of formal consensus decision-making. The summary of the secret report said "The Chair was eager to present his 'decision-making by consensus' approach. Consensus itself is not a bad thing; however, it is sometimes impossible to get consensus on difficult issues, and it is not clear how this will be handled. This is a concern."

The summary of the Secret Report concluded, "The Reviewers saw strong potential for leadership, and many ready to move the department in a positive direction, if given strong leadership." They never gave me the entire secret report, so I assume it wasn't written with the intention of developing me as a leader.

I was gutted. One of my colleagues who had accompanied me as a witness commented that that was the most hostile meeting he had ever attended on campus. I wasn't surprised: a colleague who had attended a previous meeting with me said she had never seen The Supervisor treat anyone the way she treated me. I questioned whether I had the inner strength to continue to serve my department. It was a difficult job, with or without the support from my supervisor. I was committed to continuing, but my excitement was extinguished.

The very existence of the secret report was odd. The review was meant to focus on our undergraduate programs, not my leadership. During the reviewer's visit, no one in my department mentioned my leadership nor did the reviewers ask any questions about our leadership or governance. Even commenting on the leadership of the department was unusual. For such a review to suggest that a chair be replaced was extraordinary.

The workplace investigation and the secret report seemed to be linked in their purpose. Before it was called off, The Administrator had written to The Gang of Four that she would combine the secret report with the results of the workplace investigation. Her actions appeared to be coordinated toward her goal. It was nearly a year later that one of my colleagues had a serendipitous conversation with one of our external reviewers at a conference. She revealed that The Administrator had had a secret meeting with our reviewers before they met with our department. The covert meeting was not on the agenda and was never disclosed to anyone in our department. No wonder she knew about the secret report before it existed.

Two years later, our department underwent another quality assurance review, this time regarding our graduate program. This time The Administrator did not meet with our reviewers in an extra-agenda meeting. This time the reviewers had nothing but positive things to say about my leadership, and they told me that they were impressed with how our department had "weathered the storm." Their official report noted the "outstanding reputation among Canadian graduate programs in psychology, with distinguished faculty and award-receiving students," the "collaborative and cross-disciplinary research environment in which student research is actively supported," and our strong commitment to "advancing DEI principles," with the program exemplifying "The university's mission to promote innovative and interdisciplinary research." What a difference a clandestine meeting makes!

Remote and Recorded

It can be dangerous to disclose when you've been misgendered.

A major anti-trans trope made apparent in Laverne Cox's 2020 "Disclosure" documentary is the idea that transgender people are deceptive. The assumption is that we are inherently deceptive because we are not who we say we are. Indignation about this deception is a socially acceptable form of transphobia. Recent research has reported that prejudice against transgender people is underpinned by the belief that we are deceptive (Totton et al., 2023). The belief, conscious or unconscious, is that if a transgender person does not disclose their gender history (and their medical, surgical, legal, and endocrinological history) this constitutes deception.

During the first week of Donald Trump's second term as president, he banned transgender troops from serving in the military, and he used the idea that being trans is necessarily dishonest to motivate this ban. Trump's order reads, "A man's assertion that he is a woman, and his requirement that others honor this falsehood, is not consistent with the humility and selflessness required of a service member."

In the wake of this ban, in March of 2025, a bill was introduced in the Texas legislature that would charge transgender people with "gender identity fraud." The bill proposed making it illegal for a trans person to update their sex markers or name on their official documents. Republican state representative Tom Oliverson described updating government documents as knowingly making "a false or misleading verbal or written statement" and proposed a punishment of two years in a state jail facility and a fine of $10,000. In Donald Trump's second term as president, anti-trans rhetoric has become visible and common, but it is not new.

It was two and a half years into my term as chair, and against all odds, I had made it to the half-way mark. I was still required to attend monthly meetings with The Supervisor despite having asked for a change in reporting structure. In attendance at one fateful January meeting were myself, The Supervisor, Human Resources, and a colleague from my department who accompanied me as a witness. We met in The Supervisor's office, which required a short walk on a crisp morning through the main quad. The four of us sat around her small round conference table on four identical chairs under her big wall-mounted screen. I faced the row of winter-bare trees that were visible outside.

The discussion was a review of my recent leadership. I surmised that the job of Human Resources was again to document my shortcomings, as attempts to remove me from my position as chair continued. We were in the first of two high-scrutiny meetings that they had scheduled just a week apart, both involving the same four people. The second meeting seemed redundant to me, so I had asked for an agenda. Human Resources told me I would not get an agenda. I would not be able to prepare.

During this mid-January meeting, I was misgendered, referred to using a feminine pronoun. Speaking about one of my colleagues, The Supervisor said, "He contacted Mel herself." I froze for a moment, wondering if the pronoun would be corrected. Would anyone at the meeting call attention to the mistake? Suggest a correction? Apologize? But no one intervened, and the pronoun stunk up the air as the meeting continued. After the meeting, my colleague privately asked me what he could have done to support me in that instant. I said he could have offered a correction if he was comfortable doing so.

Following the meeting Human Resources sent me the expected email detailing my failings. Referring to the compassion my departmental colleagues required from their leader, she said, "It appears to me that you may not be entirely comfortable in this space." In fact, having compassionate conversations with people in distress is one of my strengths and something that I had been doing regularly since I became chair of a department in crisis. Was Human Resources just padding her dossier of complaints about me?

I usually don't respond to these emails. I struggled to understand how conversations with Human Resources would help me grow in leadership. I hadn't been able to discern what leadership philosophy she followed, and I never thought she was delivering actionable feedback. But this email made me think that she wasn't aware of the important work I was doing in my department, and I'll admit, it bothered me that my work wasn't being acknowledged. So, I let her know that "I am very comfortable having caring and compassionate conversations. Indeed, my compassionate leadership is why I have been so successful in chairing my department. I became chair at a time when my department was in distress, and my success as a leader has created a space for healing and allowed people to refocus on the mission and vision of the department." I also mentioned that I had been misgendered during the meeting.

Human Resources denied that I had been misgendered. She told me "I am very concerned to see your allegation below and further concerned that you may misrepresent [The Supervisor's] actions again in future meetings." Later, the university's legal team told me that the misgendering "is refuted by written confirmation from another person who attended, stating that no misgendering by [The Supervisor] occurred." My email, in which I said that I was misgendered, together with Human Resource's written denial, saying that it never happened, is now part of my permanent record. My file makes it appear that I lie about being misgendered.

The retribution was swift and came from above. I received an email from The Administrator saying that "your working relationship with [The Supervisor] may no longer be tenable and ... an escalated level of intervention is required." She continued, "Recent events have illustrated that the relationship between you and [The Supervisor] has deteriorated further and is now clearly untenable. Having received advice following these recent events, I have determined that further changes to communication are required ...." The advice that The Administrator received, not coincidentally, was from Human Resources, who had sworn that I had not been misgendered.

Going forward, I was no longer going to report to The Supervisor but would be reporting to an associate dean. I received an email from this associate dean saying that he was going "to shift these meetings to an online format and record our meetings." Furthermore, both he and I would be accompanied by another person "to help facilitate discussion or raise any issues and concerns." My personal assistant, who sits at a desk about 20 ft from my desk, laughed out loud. She could not comprehend why they were going to such extraordinary measures to isolate me. This would be an extraordinary increase in surveillance and scrutiny. Other department chairs met privately, in person, without being recorded.

A good friend of mine was the president of our faculty association, and she tried to intervene on my behalf. The Administrator told her that I was being recorded in order to protect me. I was not provided with any information about who would store the recordings, how long the recordings would be retained, or who would have access to them. Although I didn't anticipate misspeaking during a meeting, I was particularly vulnerable: I had received a letter from the university's lawyer saying that I would be sued if I defamed anyone. That was a couple months after I received a letter from the same university lawyer telling me that if I were sued for defamation, the university would not defend me.

None of these remedies, being recorded, meeting only online, everyone bringing support people, were remedies that I had asked for. In fact, I hadn't even filed an official complaint following the meeting. These were not accommodations. They were restraints. I felt I was being treated as if I were a monster. People couldn't be in the same room as me and would need someone there to protect them from me, despite the fact that the meeting was remote. In addition to being under scrutiny, I was now seen as dangerous. The message was clear: I was a problem to be managed.

But a member of my department was friends with the associate dean that I was to report to, and she went to talk to him one-on-one. She told him that I was a good leader, a good chair, and a good person. She explained that this suggested meeting format was othering. She explained that the practices that were in place for other chairs should be those used with me. He understood that this treatment of me was inhumane, and he followed up his email with an invitation to come to his office and meet in person. I responded that this invitation felt very welcoming, and our monthly meetings took place in his office. I was grateful for his compassion and for the intervention of my colleague.

Denying that someone has been misgendered is not kind. If I hadn't had a witness accompanying me, I would be left to question my own perceptions, the very definition of gaslighting. I know when I have been misgendered, and I am harmed when someone formally attests that it didn't happen, creating the impression that I am a liar. This predicament is unique to transgender employees.

Another anti-trans trope is that transgender people are difficult to deal with in the workplace. We are bothersome. From accessible washrooms to databases that allow gender or name updates, even just asking to be addressed using our pronouns, our needs are treated as a burden. If we speak up about being misgendered or harassed, we're seen as overreacting or making frivolous complaints. The idea that trans people are bothersome, disruptive, or demanding has real consequences: 82% of transgender employees surveyed reported that they had been passed over for promotion, fired, or harassed because of their gender or sexual orientation (Sears et al., 2024). Because I was misgendered, I was seen as bothersome.

After Human Resources denied that I had been misgendered, I was suddenly being monitored, scrutinized, and reported on. And then I was cut off from all meaningful communication with the sexual violence office.

Reprisal

While our department was searching for a chair, a "summary of opportunities" had been circulated by the dean's office, saying "The Chair will need to manage relationships across the University, including with the DEI Office." This directive was fully consistent with my belief that open lines of communication facilitate good leadership. As chair, I networked with many people across campus, and I made it a point to network with the DEI office.

During my time as chair, I became friends with the sexual violence prevention education manager who worked in the campus sexual violence office. He was in charge of consent education on campus, which he sometimes delivered in drag. He came to my class every year to talk to our department's second-year students about consent, and we occasionally went to the campus pub together after work.

I had recently attended a discussion that he had organized for transgender members of the community, and I had left early because I had to get home and cook dinner for my family. He noticed that I had slipped out of the meeting early and emailed me the next day. "Just wanted to ensure everything was okay. Happy to connect if needed." So thoughtful. We arranged a coffee date. Two days later, a much more formal sounding email canceled our date. "My colleague has been designated as your single point of contact in the office to ensure our best service, as he is the Senior Human Rights Advisor." I responded, "We'll catch up soon," but of course that was the last time we arranged to meet on campus, and the last time we emailed using our university accounts. His boss had composed that email and had told him that he was no longer allowed to speak to me.

Less than a year into my term, the university hired a new director in the sexual violence office. I was the first person to email her to welcome her to the university. I invited her to have a cup of coffee, and we sat in a coffee shop across the street from the university during her very first week on the job. We excitedly talked about the work in her domain. Months later, she asked me out to lunch because she was beginning to understand that something unusual had happened to my department. I shared with her what I knew.

Later that year, the university hired a new Director of Human Rights, and again, I reached out to welcome her. I walked across the beautiful central quad on a cold day in mid-December and met with her in her stately stone office. I asked her about her vision for the role and offered to help her in any way I could. I made it clear that I thought it was important that we create open lines of communication between her office and my department.

Half a year after that, the university hired a new vice provost of DEI, who became the boss of these three employees. As you probably can anticipate, I emailed him on his first day on campus. I welcomed him to campus and asked him for a meeting. In our hour-long meeting, I made sure he knew that it was important to me that our offices had open lines of communication.

I am no longer allowed to talk to any of these people. There is no one in the sexual violence office that I am allowed to contact, and I have restricted access to the wider DEI office. I can only contact one designated person, and even then, there are strict conditions: I have to submit a complaint form detailing the issue and have a university lawyer present during every conversation. These were people I had welcomed when they were hired, colleagues I had met with to foster open lines of communication as recommended by the "summary of opportunities" document.

Why am I restricted? Because I had filed a complaint. The university's lawyer wrote, "Dr. Rutherford's frequent complaints underscore the importance of involving additional individuals." In the 24 years that I have been employed, I have made one complaint at the university, and yet I was being treated as if I were a font of frivolous accusations.

The networking that I was so intentional about was also used to justify my restricted access to the DEI Office. The university's lawyer wrote, "Dr. Rutherford contacts the new Vice-President of DEI directly for a meeting," as if this were— what? A violation of some policy? A waste of his time? A foray into a sacred domain, above my rank? It wasn't. It was leadership. It was networking. It was an attempt to start a conversation about making the university a safer place to work and study.

This reprisal was not just an inconvenience; it was a professional roadblock. I could no longer seek guidance on difficult conversations within my department—on issues of race, religion, or gender—conversations that cisgender chairs routinely handle with the support of the DEI Office. I could no longer invite guest speakers to my classes. Previously, I had arranged for the sexual violence prevention education manager to speak to second-year students about consent. Now, I had to rely on staff in my department to make those arrangements, a small but telling sign of the toll this stereotype was taking on my leadership. This was more than exclusion. It was a message: I was a problem to be managed, not a leader to be supported.

I can't contact the office to provide input on policies that are under development. The office has asked for broad input into policies that are being updated, including the sexual violence policy and the discrimination and harassment policy. These policy updates are of interest to me and to others in my department following the events of 2020, and these were the policies that I had promised our students we would revisit in my back-to-school email. Before I was misgendered by The Supervisor, I had attended a meeting to discuss the update of these policies, but my misgendering had somehow shifted me to a different category. Instead of being seen as a university leader who warrants a seat at the table during policy discussions, I am now a victim, stigmatized by my need to access the types of services this office provides. My colleagues can express their opinions, but I am no longer allowed to.

This reprisal was deeply isolating. The very networking and open communication that had been praised as essential leadership qualities became grounds for suspicion and exclusion. This experience revealed how harmful stereotypes about transgender people—not just in general, but specifically in leadership roles—can undermine trust, block access to vital resources, and erode one's ability to lead effectively. It was a stark reminder that combating such stereotypes requires not only personal resilience but also institutional change to create truly inclusive environments where all leaders can thrive.

Was This All About Transphobia?

While I was living through my deteriorating relationship with The Supervisor, the attempts to remove me as chair, the threat of a workplace investigation, and receiving the secret report, I was perplexed. Colleagues told me that they had never seen anyone treated this way. I didn't even know people were treated this way. There have been moments in my life when other people's treatment of me could only be explained by transphobia. This was not one of those moments.

Clearly, some of what was happening was specific to my gender. I would likely not have been misgendered if I had not transitioned. Then I would not have a letter in my file denying that I was misgendered, creating the impression that I am deceptive. And I would not have been excluded from the university's DEI office. The idea that meetings with me had to be remote and recorded would never have been suggested if it weren't for the fact that I had been misgendered. The university's mishandling of my needs was institutional transphobia. But what about the assumption that I was harming students, or the assumption that I would exclude women from the strategic plan (or even that I would want to)? Could all of the coordinated hostility be explained by transphobia?

My mind swarmed with hypotheses about why my university had turned on me. Perhaps the tarnished reputation of the department had just been transferred to me. Now that I was the leader of this department, I was going to be held responsible for any perceived or real misconduct, despite the fact that all investigations had been resolved before I became chair. Even prior to my becoming chair, the administration had given the department a cold shoulder. Trust had been broken. This was likely due to the president ordering a systemic review and not due to transphobia. The chair at the time was cisgender.

A second possibility was that the administration was under explicit and public pressure to deal with what were perceived as student-generated claims of sexual misconduct. Relatedly, the administration was swamped with legalistic concern about liability, taking the direction of their legal team for every decision. That might make the administration wary of anyone who voiced support for my department, never mind that my job included advocating for my department. Before and throughout my term as chair, this pressure was context for the administration's behavior.

A third possibility is that the administration was deeply clueless. At the highest levels of the administration, there is a lot to manage and a lot of moving parts. I imagine that at most universities, the upper administration has only the vaguest idea what happens inside departments, if they have any at all. In our case, our university got a new provost just three weeks before the systemic review of my department was ordered. She knew none of us.

A fourth possibility is that the administration wanted to sweep the whole incident under the rug, and I kept wanting to direct their attention to it. Their public criticism of me said that we weren't aligned. Holding different strategic intentions is not transphobia, but maybe their failure to share their strategic intentions with me was transphobia. I wasn't invited into the inner circle.

Over the last several years, I've had plenty of time to consider these possibilities. Indeed, they live rent free in my head. I won't try to convince you that the university's treatment of me was related to transphobia, but I will share with you that I believe it was. Certainly, all of the above hypotheses are plausible, and certainly events don't have singular causes. All of those factors influenced my term as chair. But if I had not transitioned, I believe that more information would have been shared with me, I would have been invited to explain my approach rather than disciplined for it, I would have been trusted more, and The Supervisor would not have said to me, "Imagine what it would be like to be a woman in that department." I know my gender makes some people uncomfortable because I am not as they expect. Some might find me interesting, but some find me inscrutable or confusing. That particular form of transphobia has people withdraw trust or see me with suspicion.

In order to see the impact of being in a Glass Cliff leadership position, we can compare how I was treated at my university to the treatment of a cisgender chair in a similar situation at another university. Dartmouth's psychology department also weathered highly publicized accusations of sexual assault. Nine members of the psychology department made claims of sexual assault and harassment and later won a lawsuit against the university claiming that the department had an "entrenched culture of power and abuse". In the wake of these events, an old friend of mine stepped into the position of chair at Dartmouth. Like me, he took over a department in crisis, but his was not a Glass Cliff situation. He is a tall cisgender white man. His experience of leading a department in crisis, especially his administration's treatment of him, was different from mine.

While we were both serving as chair of our recovering departments, we went to lunch and compared notes. He told me he felt supported by his administration. The leadership at his university understood that in order to get the department back to work, they would have to collaborate with the department leadership, provide support specific to getting the department back on its feet, and not battle the department chair. He did not experience the kind of scrutiny I experienced. He was treated with trust and respect. No one tried to remove him from his role. The contrast between his experience and mine illuminates the Glass Cliff phenomenon.

The Impact of Being a Glass Cliff Leader

Through these challenges, my colleagues in the department were incredibly supportive. They stood by me. They believed in the work I was doing. But the broader university was unwilling—or unable—to support my leadership. While senior leaders made public statements about inclusion, they were not willing to make my workplace safe. They announced reintegration, but no one reached out to me about how to manage that reintegration. I was left alone to figure it out. Not only was the upper administration not going to help me succeed in the unimaginable task, but I was also going to be under unrelenting scrutiny while I tried. They let me teeter on the Glass Cliff.

I do not see a path for promotion to higher leadership at my university. In hindsight, this was not a leadership opportunity, it was a containment strategy. I hadn't been given the tools to succeed. I'd been given just enough rope to hang myself. This is what it means to be offered a seat at the table—but only after the table has caught fire. My struggle illuminates the urgent need for institutions not just to proclaim values but to actively dismantle the systemic barriers that undermine true inclusivity.

One recurrent issue that I faced when I became a Glass Cliff leader was the simultaneous refusal to share information with me and a persistent failure to appreciate that I needed any information they had that would be relevant to my work. In the same meeting when the President told me that I would not be receiving any of the reports, he told me, "As you take over, the first part of this is going to be about looking at all of the information that's been put in front of you and making decisions about what is the best way to move that department forward." The Supervisor told me, "Imagine what it would be like to be a woman" without sharing with me any concerns she had heard from women. When I asked The Administrator, "There have been concerns that we're withdrawing academic support from students?" her reply was "You're aware of what's happening." The leadership simultaneously refused to share their concerns with me and expected me to address their concerns. They did not appear to see the contradiction.

Scrutiny directly interfered with my ability to do my job. At one point, I was reprimanded by The Supervisor because a faculty member had attended our faculty meeting while on leave. I was very new at my job and didn't understand the differences between all of the different types of leaves, so I sent an email to the seven other chairs asking for more information. Do faculty on leave attend faculty meetings? The Supervisor was furious. The university's lawyer wrote, "Dr. Rutherford contacted other Department Chairs ... his act was both inappropriate and out of his scope of duties as Chair." A question that any new chair might reasonably ask became, in their framing, evidence of misconduct.

The emotional impact of the scrutiny and The Administrator's meetings with me had an effect on my ability to do my job. I had come into the position with a vision and determination. People needed me, and I believed I could help people. I answered a calling. Emotionally, my term as chair can be divided into before and after The Administrator tried to remove me. Gone were the vigor and confidence. I was forced to confront my vulnerability. For a couple of years, I didn't sleep well, which made it even more difficult for me to focus on the complex tasks I was facing. Sleep brought nightmares.

Why didn't my superiors understand what a great job I was doing? I was crushed to realize that my superiors didn't appreciate the effectiveness of my leadership, and their unbridled attempt to force me out was painful and confusing. A workplace investigation is not a microaggression.

I also feared that my professional reputation and my career were under threat. As the university developed their plan for a workplace investigation, a colleague of mine warned me that a workplace investigation will always yield an unflattering critique of its target. A critical report was what the university was paying for. I feared that my job was in jeopardy. I've spent decades building up my research lab and a body of work that has deepened our understanding of social perception, the impact of social categorization on how we see people, and the development of such social perception. Would I be able to continue doing this work at my university?

These experiences exposed a painful paradox at the heart of institutional leadership: the very qualities I brought—inclusivity, collaboration, and a commitment to open communication—were questioned not on their merits, but because my leaders disliked me. Even in nominally progressive spaces like universities, institutional transphobia operates quietly but ruthlessly. What happens when a trans leader is cast as a threat? I wasn't developed—I was contained.

I spent my 55th birthday on the university's website trying to figure out when I could retire.

Yet, despite the rebuke and the offer of an administrative leave, this onslaught reaffirmed my resolve to lead authentically. I wanted to remain chair of my department for the duration of my five-year term. I had stepped into a Glass Cliff leadership position because I felt called. I had committed to a five-year term because I thought my department needed that stability while we were re-building our foundations. True leadership requires courage—to keep showing up, to stand firm in one's values, even when challenged by power. This treatment underscored the urgent need for institutions to prepare for leaders who embody diverse experiences and perspectives.

I had committed to using a values-based approach to leading the department and the department was rebuilding. I wanted to invest in shared leadership. I felt the need to encourage my colleagues to participate in university governance. And I wanted to call people in, rather than calling people out. It was worth riding out the storm and holding a steadfast commitment to my values.

At the end of the day, it turned out that my university has no policy or procedure for the removal of a department chair.

References

Sears, B., Mallory, C., Lin, A., & Castleberry, N. M. (2024). *Workplace experiences of transgender employees*. UCLA School of Law, Williams Institute.

Totton, R. R., Rios, K., & Shogren, N. (2023). Distrusted disclosures: deception drives anti-transgender but not anti-atheist prejudice. *Frontiers in Psychology, 13*, 1006107. https://doi.org/10.3389/fpsyg.2022.1006107

7

Shared Leadership: Just the Support I Needed

I needed help. The complexities of my situation were overwhelming. If I was going to succeed in my leadership, I was going to need to develop shared leadership. The Administrator controlled the university's purse strings. Our department was going to need help, including financial help, to get back to our previous level of research productivity. Our publication rate had declined while allegations were being publicized. When people were forbidden to speak to their students, students were reassigned to other supervisors and some of their research never got published. Years after the investigations were complete, we still weren't firing on all cylinders. We rely on our students' efforts to maintain the kind of research productivity that attracts grant support, but we need grant money in order to accept graduate students. People were struggling to get back on the hamster wheel.

One rainy afternoon, a colleague invited me and our current associate chair of research to her home. We had planned to have a walking meeting, but with the rain increasing in intensity, we had a cup of tea and watched the world get drenched instead. From the warmth of her living room, we created a proposal and a budget.

Our host for the afternoon was particularly creative in proposing solutions. She was determined to find ways to get people back to research. Part of her proposal was to hire postdoctoral fellows whose research interests were connected to multiple labs and who could therefore inspire collaborations. She also thought we could hire a public relations consultant who would create a publicity campaign for our department in an attempt to salvage our reputation to make us more attractive to both students and granting agencies. Her proposal also included hiring a strategist to work directly with our colleagues who were trying to write grant applications. All of these were great ideas, but all of them were going to cost money. We agreed that I should not be the one to ask The Administrator for resources since she did not seem motivated to help me succeed as a leader. And I was scared of her.

I needed shared leadership. I needed to enroll my colleagues to do the work that would normally be the role of the department chair: advocating for the needs of the department to the upper administration. The next week, I stood in the chair's office and watched these two colleagues walk up the university's quad to the old stone building where The Administrator was ready to meet them. I was full of gratitude. These two colleagues had known me since before I transitioned and they wanted me to succeed. They wanted our department to succeed, and they understood that I needed help. My colleagues were partially successful: The Administrator provided some money to hire three postdoctoral fellows. A Glass Cliff leader may need help in serving as their organization's advocate.

Why Shared Leadership?

Shared leadership is not just about jointly constructing your processes; it is about jointly constructing your goals and purpose. Pearce and Conger defined shared leadership as "a dynamic interactive influence process among individuals in groups for which the objective is to lead one another to the achievement of group or organizational goals" (Pearce & Conger, 2003, p. 1). Shared leadership is not just a delegation of tasks, it involves shared power, shared decision-making, shared vision, and shared responsibility. Shared leadership includes influence and collaboration between peers, the leader's influence on others in the organization, and influence by anyone in the organization on the leader. Leadership is broadly distributed through an organization, not just reserved for the nominal leader. The person sitting in the executive role both listens to colleagues and invites colleagues to participate in leadership. Many or perhaps most people in the organization can show up as a leader. Shared leadership means that the person who holds the executive role is not alone in leading the organization.

Carson and colleagues reported evidence that the result of adopting a shared leadership strategy is greater performance throughout the team (Carson et al., 2007). This is because people develop the sense that they have agency. If people feel that they can impact the organization and they feel that the organization can therefore support their own goals and values, then they have more investment in the organization and more ownership of their own work. The result is higher morale and higher productivity. With power and responsibility, people are more committed to success. According to Peter Northouse, "Teams with shared leadership have less conflict, more consensus, more trust, and more cohesion" (Northouse, 2025).

As Carson and colleagues point out, a team is ready to try shared leadership if they have shared purpose and all the people on the team feel like they have a voice (Carson et al., 2007). Once we had articulated our core values and our mission and vision statement, we knew our shared purpose. We were using consensus decision-making and strategizing at faculty meetings about how to open channels of communication so that all voices could be heard. People were leaving space for quiet voices and explicitly creating multiple channels of communication. We were ready for shared leadership.

During my term, I have noticed several advantages of shared leadership. I was able to benefit from the wisdom of my predecessors. We developed a roster of people with leadership skills, so we were ready for succession planning. We were able to engage in strategic planning together, and information about our processes became widely understood. Given that I needed help from my colleagues, I found that shared leadership makes Glass Cliff leadership possible.

The Wisdom of Previous Leaders

When people take turns being department chair, as we do in my department, an emergent benefit is that you accumulate past chairs. Former leaders can be a fantastic asset to the organization, lending their wisdom and experience when asked. When I served as chair, we had three former chairs in the department and a retired former chair who lived in an adjacent neighborhood. All of them were helpful to me, explaining how the multiple budgets in the department work (it's complicated), explaining the history of our fifteen undergraduate programs, and deciphering the intentions of some administrator. I could not have done what I did without them.

My predecessor was chair when allegations were unfolding and when most of the public communication about our department was being released by the administration. He had tried to communicate to the administration about our concerns but got the cold shoulder. They were no longer interested in hearing his concerns once they had ordered a review of our department's culture. He bore the brunt of the administration's behavior as he pleaded for help and watched the impact on our department.

When I became chair, and on several occasions early in my term as chair, this predecessor told me that the department was mine now. He made it clear that he was fully prepared to support my vision. At one point, about a year and a half into my term as chair, we were preparing to meet with the mediator who was handling our grievance negotiations with the university administration. I had been working closely with my predecessor to clarify our values and goals ahead of this mediation. I thought we were going into the meeting as partners. But as the date approached, he told me that I needed to take the lead. Because I was the chair, I had to be very clear what my vision was and what my desired outcomes were. He told me that I needed to negotiate with the mediator, and he was just there to support me if needed. I was horrified. I had to do this? But he was right, and I was able to get very clear on my values and what our department needed to achieve during mediation. I took the lead, and he was in the room with me.

When The Administrator was trying to remove me using the $226,000 deficit in our graduate budget as one of her reasons, our former leaders rescued me. Our department had always been fiscally responsible. Just months before I became chair, our budget had a healthy surplus. We had a number of problems, but the budget wasn't one. I didn't understand where the deficit came from. I asked our department manager, and her forensic accounting revealed that this was money spent to support the graduate students whose supervisors had been forbidden from contacting or supporting them. I turned to my predecessor and our former associate chair of graduate studies, the two department leaders who had dealt with our graduate students during the upheaval. They told me that our dean had not only authorized these payments but also promised to reimburse the department. They went through years-old emails and found the communications that made it clear that the department would not be left holding the debt. Emails in hand, I asked our dean to cover these costs. Because I had the support of my former department leaders, I was able to show promises that these costs would be covered. She told me that I should have asked her years ago, when I became chair, and at this point, this was "a new ask." The department was eventually reimbursed, and I didn't lose my job.

Another example of support I got from a former chair was when The Administrator hired a Workplace Investigation law firm to investigate my leadership in an attempt to remove me as chair. I needed help making sense of what was going on. I went to see a former chair. This time, I didn't go to my predecessor, I went four chairs back.

This Maritimer had been chair decades ago when I was hired. She had spent her whole career at our university. In addition to her terms as chair, she served on the university's board of governors and senate as well as leading our faculty association. She knew everyone and she knew every policy. She is retired, but she lives so close that when my kids were little, we always went to her house to trick-or-treat. She has a big personality and is a powerhouse of a leader. She's seen every trick in the book.

I hadn't seen her in years, but I emailed to ask her for a conversation. She invited me to her home. One sunny April afternoon, the worst April of my life, I walked the 20 minutes from campus to her house. She made me tea and served me the Christmas cookies she had taken out of her freezer. We sat in her living room, she in her favorite chair, and me in the guest spot on the couch.

As I told her my story, she quickly understood why I needed her perspective. She expressed the appropriate outrage at how I was being treated, and she told me to be strong. She told me to stick to my values. She explained that the upper administration often didn't know what was going on at the department level. She said the important thing was that I had the complete support of our entire department, including her. She believed that I was helping the department, that I was doing brave things, and that the department wanted me to continue to lead. In addition to being extremely knowledgeable, she was also kind and compassionate. She told me to get back to work. It was the only time I sought her counsel during my term, and I was glad she was in my corner.

I look forward to being a supportive former chair. I'm picturing myself as the Jimmy Carter of our department.

Built in Succession Planning

A recurrent challenge in academia is finding someone to chair the department. Generally, academics are excited about their research and engaged in their teaching, and serving as chair will disrupt these endeavors. Shared leadership is a great strategy to develop a pool of people who have practiced their leadership skills and have enough insight into how the organization is run to make an informed decision when it is time for a new leader. Broadly engaging the team in shared leadership results in a pool of qualified people who could step into leadership. Without a deep leadership bench, the organization may have a difficult time identifying the next leader or may have a difficult transition when an inexperienced leader is appointed.

Having experienced leaders among the team will benefit the organization if the leader takes a leave or just goes on vacation. An organization with shared leadership, with deliberately developed leaders, is both ready for a crisis and ready to seize any opportunities for growth and expansion. If you nurture leaders broadly in your organization, you'll have reserves. If not, a leader may feel unable to step down, seeing that no one else is ready to take over. I was pretty committed to making sure someone was ready to take over by the time my term finished.

Before I was chair, our department had two associate chairs, one for our undergraduate programs and one for our graduate program. When I became chair, I created a new position, an associate chair of research. Each of the three associate chair roles has been filled by two different people during my term, which means that six people have served as associate chair during my five-year term. Each of these six were new to departmental leadership. I could have chosen people who were senior to me, or people who were experienced associate chairs, but I chose six colleagues who had never held leadership positions in the department before. They are all very capable people who had expressed an interest in leadership, and now they have leadership experience in the department. They have insight into the workings of the department, and others in the department have had a chance to see them as leaders. From their associate chair position, they could step up to the role of chair or even step up a level to a dean or associate dean position.

I was determined to support these colleagues as they stepped into leadership roles. I created a leadership curriculum for the associate chairs that I delivered throughout my five-year term. We met quarterly as a group to discuss specific topics and associated readings. Early in my term I checked in with them about what topics would be useful, and then I did some research to find best practices and a useful reading for each topic. Topics covered have included accountability and feedback, conflict resolution and mediation, goal setting, strategic planning, hiring, and how to plan and facilitate a meeting. Each time we met, we would read a chapter or an article on the topic, and we would discuss it over lunch. Of course, we also talked about happenings in the department, and we talked about our kids and our vacations, but the whole group actually did the reading, and we had rich discussions about these leadership topics.

On one occasion, our topic of discussion was feedback, and we talked about developing the skills of both receiving and giving feedback. We discussed what worked and what didn't work in our own experiences. Then my colleagues surprised me by asking me for feedback. They specifically wanted critical feedback. Although I had often thanked them for their work and pointed out their successes, they suspected that maybe I was being too nice. They wondered if they were losing out on an opportunity for development because I was hesitant to criticize their work. Instead of giving them a quick answer over lunch, I told them I would think about it. Later I privately gave them the direction that I thought would be most helpful to support their professional development and lead them to success in their role as well as any future leadership role.

Creating Shared Information

Calling people into shared leadership and working elbow to elbow with them will lead to a broader understanding of the processes your organization uses. Like many organizations, our department reviews faculty members' performance annually. Faculty members report on their teaching, research, and service and the department evaluates their job performance and recommends a pay increase.

As you can imagine, it is very helpful for faculty members to have insight into how this evaluation happens. A faculty member who knows what is being evaluated will be better able to allocate their time during the academic year and to use their annual report to showcase their work. To this end, I decided that I wanted to include as many people as possible in the evaluation process.

Each year, I gathered a group of three faculty members to work with me to evaluate the reports that faculty members have turned in and then discuss the merit of each person's job performance. Each year, it was a different group of three people. At the beginning of my five-year term, I mapped out who would join me each year in our annual review of faculty performance, ensuring that no one joined the group more than once, and therefore maximizing the number of people who are included in this process. I made sure that the three people represented different ranks and different specializations. By the time my term as chair was over, more than half of the faculty members in my department had an opportunity to see how the sausage was made.

I could see evidence that the understanding of this process was spreading. During my term I saw a shift in the way our faculty members prepared their report on their activities for the year. For example, they came to understand that the section describing teaching activities was particularly important and became much more detailed in their descriptions of how they improve their teaching, update their content, and respond to student feedback. Shared leadership leads to transparency and shared, actionable information.

Shared Leadership Leaves You Nimble

Shared leadership allows the organization to share not just the impact of leadership but also the workload. It saves the leader time. I've watched leaders who micromanage and who cannot commit to passing a task to a colleague without staying directly involved. In order to foster shared leadership, you have to not micromanage. That may not be easy. If you are an experienced leader, you might be able to do a task faster and more efficiently than the person you passed it to, but don't. Once you are clear that a member of your organization understands the task, let them have a shot at succeeding. While it is always good to check in and offer support, don't take the job back just because you've gotten impatient. Let people learn and let them succeed. Employees appreciate feeling trusted to do their jobs. Employees who feel micromanaged don't feel trusted, which can be frustrating.

I have found that trusting my colleagues to plan and to execute the work of the department frees up my time. This delegation leaves me more nimble in the event that something unexpected requires my attention. In my fourth year as chair, our department was preparing for an external review of our graduate program. This involved writing an 80-page "self-study" in which we describe our program, its requirements, its objectives, the faculty who serve it, and our successes and aspirations. It is a lot of work.

This document would normally be prepared by the associate chair of graduate studies. Right as we moved into the months during which we would normally be finishing this document, our associate chair of graduate studies stepped down, and I invited another colleague to fill the position. The new associate chair had to learn this new position at a time of year when we were interviewing the next incoming class, and I thought asking him to create our self-study at the same time would be too much. I wanted to ease him into the position. Because our department has a practice of shared leadership, I actually had the capacity to take on a task which normally would not be the responsibility of the chair. We got the self-study finished on time and the reviewers had it by the expected date. They gave us a glowing review.

As another example of my availability, I was able to pick up the task of creating a promotion dossier for a colleague. As chair, I had prioritized the professional development of my colleagues—I wanted to move them up through the ranks. There were a number of faculty members in my department who were not tenured or were not yet at the rank of full professor, so they had promotions in their future. I met with each of these colleagues a couple of times a year to talk about what they needed to do to prepare for their promotion. When they were eligible, I encouraged them to go up for promotion. I was so successful in talking people into preparing and going up for promotion that in my fourth year, our department had seven cases to prepare. I benefited from shared leadership by having most of the senior members of the department participate in preparing promotion cases. This meant that more than half the faculty members in the department came to understand how to prepare a promotion case. It also meant that I had time to step in and take over an extra case when we learned about it late in the game. Shared leadership left me nimble enough to pick up the emergent workload.

Strategic Planning

We were able to use our strategic planning process to make shared leadership and leadership development visible throughout the department. Our strategic planning supported shared leadership in two distinct ways. First, the process of creating the strategic plan was itself an act of shared leadership since everyone had a seat at the table and could see that they were impacting the trajectory of the department. Second, the strategic plan we created named shared leadership and leadership development as explicit goals.

In my first year as chair, the entire department engaged in ten months of strategic planning which resulted in a five-year strategic plan. The Strategic Planning Committee was made up of nine faculty members, who represented a variety of research areas, levels of seniority, and genders. The committee started by organizing a day-long faculty and staff retreat. The committee planned the format and the discussions for this retreat, and our professional facilitator, Darlene Chrissley, led us through a series of reflections. We considered prompts such as "The best of who we are and what we bring," "Imagine our department in the future," "research," "teaching," "internal community," "external community," and "What action should we prioritize?" Notes from this session were shared with the department. The Strategic Planning Committee met to identify major themes that should be included in the five-year plan.

Over the next couple of months, the department developed the core values statement that was foundational to our strategic plan, and the Strategic Planning Committee wrote our Mission and Vision Statement. Meanwhile, over a three-month period, members of the Strategic Planning Committee met with graduate students in a series of 8 roundtable meetings. Every graduate student was invited to each roundtable, and multiple email reminders were sent in order to encourage participation. The purpose was to get input relevant to the graduate program section of the plan as well as to the strategic plan in general. Each roundtable meeting had a different prompt, for example, "Fostering a culture of positive communication" and "Exciting new directions in our research field."

In a second faculty retreat, we began our discussions about the next faculty members we wanted to hire. What area of research did we want to grow? We ensured that we had broad conversations across the faculty members in the department: We worked in small groups to create possible job descriptions. Then all of the job descriptions were taped to the walls for a "dotmocracy" exercise: each person had six dots to stick to any job description they liked. Job descriptions were later transcribed into a document, listed in the order from the most dots to the least dots.

We held four faculty roundtables. Faculty members met in four groups of eight people to discuss our vision and the direction we wanted to grow. The drafts from the recent faculty retreat were a starting point. In order to break down silos and encourage engagement across the department, the four groups were not created based on any predescribed areas but were the group of faculty members that were available when each meeting was scheduled: two on Zoom and two in person.

We then circulated the notes from all four faculty roundtables to our faculty members and I met with the associate chair of research to compile a draft of our potential next hires. The draft was sent to the Strategic Planning Committee for comment and then circulated to all faculty members for comment. These processes were designed very intentionally by our Strategic Planning Committee to ensure that the planning process was inclusive.

Our strategic five-year plan lists leadership development among our goals. "Developing leaders within our department who are skilled at promoting our core values allows us to assist each other in creating safe spaces for constructive communication. Moreover, developing a number of leaders in the spirit of succession planning helps maintain the community founded on our Core Values into the future."

Leadership development was so important that the introductory table that listed our goals said, "A goal of this five-year plan is to 'Skill Up' in the area of leadership and increase our participation in all levels of university governance." We included subsections of the plan called "Skill Building" and "Leadership Development."

Our strategic plan describes our plan to mentor new faculty members: "We have a long tradition of assigning new members to one or two more senior mentors in our department." This mentorship scheme both signals our collective commitment to developing one another and distributes the mentorship opportunities broadly.

One of the explicit goals that we listed in our strategic plan was "to develop leadership in our department so that new leaders have the skills and values to grow our departmental culture in the future." We stated:

> We will engage a coach trainer to teach us coaching skills. Coaching skills will help us to engage in "Calling in" rather than "Calling out," following the teachings of Dr. Loretta Ross. We will learn and practice these skills at faculty retreats, and staff and faculty members will have an opportunity to use these skills in their leadership and mentorship activities.

We signaled our intention to increase transparency and deep understanding of our processes through shared leadership:

> When tenure and promotion study groups are formed, people who have not served before will be considered, and people who have served but not chaired before will be given the opportunity to chair. Each year a different group will advise the chair on annual reviews, and that advisory group will include Assistant and Associate level faculty. Committee membership will be reviewed annually. Leadership workshops offered at the University will be advertised within the department and participation will be supported.

My favorite line in our strategic plan comes from the summary of our description of how we were going to rebuild our community. We said, "We are imperfect, forgiving, and committed to continuous improvement."

Name It Leadership

In order to develop leaders in the department, I acknowledge people when I see them taking on leadership roles. It is a simple leadership-development strategy: When you see someone acting as a leader, tell them that what they are doing is leadership, whether they are in a formal leadership role or not. By doing so, you are inviting them to see themselves in leadership.

Early in my term, I noticed a couple of our graduate students working hard to revitalize our graduate student community. Prior to 2020, our graduate students loved the supportive community in our department. Between 2009 and 2015, the highest rated item on our graduate exit survey was "camaraderie amongst graduate students". For as long as I had been in the department, graduate students had gathered for a "Friday Social," a weekly student-led, community-building event. Given the number of people in the department who had been told that they were not allowed to communicate with each other, coupled with the rumors that were swirling around about social gatherings being policy violations, our students didn't know what they were allowed to do. Friday Social ended abruptly, and our graduate students were confused about what kinds of social events were permitted.

Since the administration had spoken publicly about alcohol, and one administrator had even given an on-camera interview to the local media attributing inappropriate behavior to alcohol (before any investigations had determined whether there was inappropriate behavior to be explained), our students were confused about whether alcohol was allowed at their gatherings. One student started organizing weekly hikes in a nearby forested area so that graduate students would have some social connections. Two students organized off-campus social events, like pizza in a local park. These events were somewhat successful until winter rolled in.

These students were not in any official leadership role. They weren't elected and they didn't have any title. But they understood the importance of building social connections among our students, and since they were among the most senior students in the department, they had experienced the collaborative and supportive culture we had had prior to 2020. They valued these gatherings and were willing to do the work to rekindle them. I made a point of thanking these students for their leadership. I wrote a letter of support when one of these students was nominated for a leadership award, which he won.

Another example involved a talk series that faculty members and students organize. As chair, it is my task to assign each faculty member committees to serve on, and I try to look at the department holistically so that everyone is contributing and everyone has opportunities to develop their leadership. One faculty member took the lead in organizing this talk series for a couple of years. The series was successful, but the faculty member was frustrated by low attendance. He sent an email to the department suggesting that the series be ended. I responded privately to his email telling him that it was okay for him to step down. I told him that while we appreciated his leadership, he wasn't the only person who could serve in this role. I told him that if it was important someone else would pick up the task. I shared the story of the old woman who was too tired to get up to make the sun rise. I specifically thanked him for his leadership. He stepped aside, and someone else took over the task of running the talk series.

It is important to name leadership when you see it. By naming it, you are validating the work. You are framing a person's efforts as a contribution to the community. You are both encouraging more of the same and inviting the person to see themselves as a leader. Perhaps such encouragement will help those people be open to accepting formal leadership roles in the future.

Developing Leaders at All Levels

In addition to the leadership curriculum that I developed for our associate chairs, I also met monthly with each of our junior faculty members, from the time we hired them until they completed the tenure process. The primary objective of these meetings was to make sure that they were aware of the requirements for tenure so that they could allocate their time and resources to prepare their tenure case. Our university has over a half a dozen policies that are relevant to the tenure process, and there are some specific things our junior faculty members can do to prepare. Publishing is the most important, and keeping notes about how they develop and implement their teaching philosophy is helpful when the tenure dossiers are assembled. I also provided support on any other issues they brought to the meeting.

Along the way, we also talked about challenges that emerged, and that usually included their leadership challenges. Each of these faculty members is in a leadership position in their own lab, mentoring students, postdocs, and research assistants. Challenges emerged when there was a mismatch between a student's skillset and their role, or if their motivation waned. I usually took a coach approach to such challenges, but I also relied on my experience as well as advice I have gotten from my mentors. We always found a solution, and my colleagues' confidence in their leadership abilities increased.

My department has managed to create not only shared leadership, but layers of leadership support. While I've been delivering a leadership curriculum to my associate chairs and to our newest faculty members, we have made explicit the value of shared leadership and leadership development.

When I had been chair for nearly two years, we hired a professional coach to work with our faculty and staff during a retreat to teach us some coaching skills. We talked about the benefits of coaching. We talked about how we could create a supportive framework in which solutions are generated. We talked about the fact that ideally the solution comes from the person being coached, while the coach asks open and insightful questions. We talked about situations in our work that might benefit from a coach approach, both in our teaching and in managing our research labs. Then we practiced our coaching skills right there in our retreat.

The result is that our community is familiar with the coach approach. We now have this skill in our toolbox to use when we are in a leadership role, helping students or other faculty members solve workplace puzzles. As a result, faculty members are more comfortable asking coaching questions, and coaching is becoming a part of our culture. We've normalized asking for help to think through challenges. I used a coach approach on a regular basis during my term as chair, and I had a coach myself during the first two years of my term.

Developing Leaders with an Eye to Inclusivity

My department is small enough that I know everyone. My department members were the people I was committed to caring for, and I actively invested in their professional development. I needed to be conscientious about providing leadership opportunities to everyone who might want them.

Everyone has implicit biases, including expectations about what a leader looks like. A stereotype about a particular group can influence whether an individual is considered for leadership. Men are more likely to become seen as leaders while they are not in leadership positions (Karau & Eagly, 1999), a phenomenon known as "leadership emergence" (Badura et al., 2018). A man is more likely to be perceived as engaged in leadership than a woman who is engaged in exactly the same activity (Scott & Brown, 2006). Ask yourself, is a woman organizing an employee appreciation lunch, engaged in leadership? What about a man engaged in the same activity? If managers don't think that an employee's gender (or race or religion) is stereotypically consistent with leadership, that employee may not be considered for leadership (Heilman, 2001; Heilman & Eagly, 2008). Neglecting to consider someone for leadership might be entirely subconscious.

Leadership is not a zero-sum game—it flourishes when it includes rather than excludes. Given that we all have biases, it would be easy for me to pick out the people who look and act like my expectation of a leader and mentor those people to become department leaders in the future. My intention was to be aware of and challenge my own narratives about who "fits" as a leader. I wanted to both reflect on the biases I held and be proactive in creating environments where leadership reflects the rich diversity of lived experiences.

One strategy I employed while developing leaders was systematically keeping track of who I had included in leadership development opportunities over time. This kind of deliberate planning can help mitigate implicit biases, and the wider the time frame the more effective it is. I had spreadsheets that tracked and quantified leadership opportunities over my five-year term, and every time I reached out and asked for help chairing a working group or serving on a hiring committee, I started by having a look at who I had asked in the past. I systematically kept track of committee membership and reached out to invite people to be engaged in the department when necessary. Without such a tracking system, I might have just picked the person I picked last time because they fit the bill or because I knew they would say yes.

Another strategy toward inclusive leadership development is to remember to ask people in your organization whether they are interested in leadership. I asked several faculty members in my department and a few of our staff members if they were interested in leadership. When opportunities came along for leadership or leadership training, I nurtured the professional development that these people wanted to engage in. If someone tells you that they are not interested in leadership development, come back in a few years and ask again. Everyone is dealing with their own priorities, family, and health, and such things can change over time.

Developing people was the heart of my job as chair. It was really important to me that I was able to include everyone in my leadership development efforts. If you want to be more inclusive, you can develop strategies that ameliorate implicit bias, especially if you have a term of several years.

Academia Is an Ideal Workplace for Shared Leadership

I found my time as chair to be rewarding work. It was really a dream leadership gig, notwithstanding the challenges that I faced as a Glass Cliff leader. Many leadership books focus on leadership in a business context, where the goal is profit, and leadership is therefore a means to that end. Leadership in a for-profit context requires some heavy lifting because you have to motivate people to increase the company's profits when that objective may not be intrinsically rewarding to employees. By comparison, shared leadership is a natural fit in academia.

In academia, the leader does not have to single-handedly create the vision and then motivate employees to get behind that vision. We all share the mission of discovery and learning, and together we build the pathways that bring our vision to life. Professors in my department have research programs that they have developed from scratch. Their inquiry and discovery are inherently motivating. Instructors in my department have a dream of engaging students and sparking curiosity. I am the leader of a department that is full of people with vision, drive, and passion. Under these circumstances, the task of leadership is straightforward: leadership involves discovering people's goals and then removing barriers and providing support that helped them meet these goals. First, create processes that allow the vision to be jointly defined. Then provide the resources and administrative support that move this vision forward. And keep the vision in view.

The fact that people have aspirations makes leadership easy: Academia is a great place to practice shared leadership.

Moving Forward

We were on our way to forging the road to repair within the department. Our culture was strong, and we were ready to support each other through our recovery and collaborate on our academic endeavors going forward. Defining our values and our shared vision accomplished two things. First, the process was healing, as we talked together about who we were and what we had to offer. Second, it was our road map out of the mire. Even as our internal operations were stabilizing, we still had to tend to the blow to our reputation. How could we manage how we were perceived from outside of the department?

References

Badura, K. L., Grijalva, E., Newman, D. A., Yan, T. T., & Jeon, G. (2018). Gender and leadership emergence: A meta-analysis and explanatory model. *Personnel Psychology, 71*(3), 335–367. https://doi.org/10.1111/peps.12266

Carson, J. B., Tesluk, P. E., & Marrone, J. A. (2007). Shared leadership in teams: An investigation of antecedent conditions and performance. *Academy of Management Journal, 50*(5), 1217–1234. https://doi.org/10.5465/amj.2007.20159921

Heilman, M. E. (2001). Description and prescription: How gender stereotypes prevent women's ascent up the organizational ladder. *Journal of Social Issues, 57*(4), 657–674. https://doi.org/10.1111/0022-4537.00234

Heilman, M. E., & Eagly, A. H. (2008). Gender stereotypes are alive, well, and busy producing workplace discrimination. *Industrial and Organizational Psychology, 1*(4), 393–398. https://doi.org/10.1111/j.1754-9434.2008.00072.x

Karau, S. J., & Eagly, A. H. (1999). Invited reaction: Gender, social roles, and the emergence of leaders. *Human Resource Development Quarterly, 10*(4), 321–327.

Northouse, P. G. (2025). *Leadership: Theory and practice.* Sage Publications.

Pearce, C. L., & Conger, J. A. (2003). All those years ago. In C. L. Pearce & J. A. Conger (Eds.), *Shared leadership: Reframing the hows and whys of leadership* (pp. 1–18). Sage Publications.

Scott, K. A., & Brown, D. J. (2006). Female first, leader second? Gender bias in the encoding of leadership behavior. *Organizational Behavior and Human Decision Processes, 101*(2), 230–242. https://doi.org/10.1016/j.obhdp.2006.06.002

8

Refusing Shame: How We Made Our Good Work Visible

During the worst of the publicity, it was difficult for us to go out in public. We were being villainized in the local press and mocked on Reddit. One faculty member was approached by a neighbor who accused him of covering up the egregious behavior that he assumed must have sparked the publicity. One of our faculty members was told by a nurse, "Oh, yeah. I've heard about what goes on in your department," as she squeezed a COVID-19 vaccination into his arm. In a graduate class a student said she did not feel safe "because of what was going on in the department," despite the fact that the class was conducted online—she had never physically been in the same room with any member of our department. One of our students was denied a job interview because of their association with our department.

The impacts of the publicity lasted for years. During the spring of 2024, I was chair of my church's ministerial search committee, and in that role, I was giving an update, speaking from the pulpit. I explained where we were in the search process by comparing it to the search for a department manager that we were conducting in our department. After the service, a congregant approached me with a smile on the verge of laughter. He told me, "I know what goes on in that department." I felt my heart sink. Four years after the university started publicizing the allegations and three years after my colleagues had been cleared and returned to work, I couldn't mention my department in town without risking mockery.

In the summer of 2024, a prospective student asked for her deposit back after she encountered old news stories about the department on the internet. In the summer of 2025, we were called "just awful" on Reddit. The reputational challenges were long-lasting and were impacting our ability to attract students. Reputation repair was a priority.

Most leaders think about the reputation of their organization. Most leaders are interested in shining the spotlight on the great work their people are doing and the accomplishments of the organization. My Glass Cliff leadership job included reputation promotion and more. Our reputation had been ruined, and we had to pull it out of the abyss before we could start building it up again.

Reclaiming Our Name

Prior to the events of 2020, our department was proud of the comfortable, collaborative culture we had created. We were proud of our student-centered focus. Suddenly we were being scrutinized and publicly criticized. This was a threat to our identity and our dignity, and as chair, I was afraid that people would feel shame and retreat.

Shame is associated with social disengagement (Brown, 2006; Scheff, 2003). Research shows that entire groups of people can be silenced by shame (Munt, 2008). One could reasonably expect the response of the department to public shaming would mirror the responses described in the psychology literature.

In some cases, shame is associated with suicide (Torres & Bergner, 2010). When the chair of Dartmouth's psychology department was accused of "enabling abuse" after a series of allegations of sexual assault in his department, he died by suicide. During the eight months when members of our department were not allowed to communicate with us, we wondered if everyone would survive long enough to reconnect.

But social disengagement is not the only response to shame. Some people respond to public shame by seeking opportunities to repair their reputation and restore their self-esteem (Silfver, 2007). This repair process is not just about updating one's own sense of self, or one's identity. Rather, it fundamentally relies on engaging with the people who hold the negative perception. The repair is a social process (Ferguson et al., 2000). From our vantage point within the department, we could see the disconnect between the culture that we had developed with care and the public narrative. In the wake of this public shaming, we did not retreat into disengagement, we actively engaged in a process of reputational repair that required vulnerability, visibility, and a deliberate effort to reclaim the narrative. Rejecting shame is a queer superpower because queer and trans people have experience defying a lifetime of societal messages that have tried to control how our identities are seen.

In a faculty meeting early in 2021, when we were just beginning to formulate a plan to repair our reputation, we contemplated making a public statement. Maybe if we just explained to a journalist that we did not condone sexual exploitation, it would clear everything up. Just hearing the idea out loud was enough for us to realize that such a course of action was unlikely to be beneficial. Who would believe us? Because of the nature of the negative publicity, we had lost the ability to make statements on our own behalf.

I made my very first attempt to raise the profile of the department just before I became chair. Once I had been selected and my appointment had gone through the governance bodies at the university, I contacted a friend of mine who was a reporter for the local newspaper. Although I had transitioned while in my current department, I had never been very vocal about being transgender. Some of my younger colleagues didn't even know I was trans. It's not that I wasn't out, it is just that I don't tend to draw a lot of attention to myself. But I wanted to show my department in a positive light, and in the moment, a news story reporting the appointment of the department's first transgender chair seemed like a step in the right direction.

The paper was interested in a story about me, and on July 9, 2021, a story was published under the title "Mel Rutherford becomes first transgender department head." The story ran with a photograph of me standing in front of the university. It said, "The acclaimed psychologist, researcher and author has been appointed chair." It went on to describe my work and some of the mentoring activities I had done on campus, like being selected the Mentor of the Month for the Women in Science and Engineering group, and delivering a talk called "Queer in Academia." In the story I described how supportive and inclusive my department had been when I transitioned. One of my most senior colleagues reached out to me to thank me, saying that she, too, thought this provided some much-needed positive publicity for the department.

Some of my friends who are not connected to the university were surprised when they saw the story. They weren't surprised that I had been appointed chair, and they weren't surprised that the local newspaper found the story newsworthy. They were surprised that I was willing to draw attention to myself and my gender. They wondered if I was doing something strategic. I was. I wanted to show my department that we did not have to retreat in shame. We could keep showing up.

Listening Up: Leadership in the Hierarchy

Effective leadership and collaboration within hierarchical institutions require intentional engagement with power. We need to both support the vision of those in leadership and also ensure that leaders actively listen to and understand us. Cultivating reciprocal understanding across ranks takes work and strategic planning.

Years ago, I had a meeting in a coffee shop with a local activist, one of the most well-known queer activists in town who is very well-connected with local leaders. She's the kind of mover and shaker who plays tennis with the mayor, even though she doesn't agree with everything he is doing. She told me that whenever she is meeting a newly elected official, a mayor, or a city council member, she starts the conversation by asking, "How can I support your leadership?" She acknowledges that a new leader will come in with a vision of their own, and she knows that in order to collaborate with this new leader, you need to work in the context of their vision.

I was surprised that this was her opening line, and I squinted at her under furrowed brows. I thought that such an influential activist would confront the new leader, presenting social justice demands and asking for support from the new leader, rather than the other way around. The idea stretched my thinking, and that conversation has impacted how I work. Unless there is a really compelling reason not to, we should support a new leader's vision and give them an opportunity to show us where they can take us.

Now I start by having a conversation with leaders, especially new leaders, to get a sense of their vision and also to offer to support their vision if I can. I have come to see myself as part of the larger whole; I'm not just a member of my department; I'm also a member of my university. I may not have a university-level leadership role, but I can still participate in university leadership.

As our department weathered the harrowing events of 2020, we had no friends in high places. No member of our department was in the upper administration or on the board of governors. We didn't have a place at the table in the university planning committee or anyone serving in a leadership role in the Faculty of Science. We were not participating in shared leadership across the university. Instead, we trusted that upper administrators knew how to run the university and would provide us with a safe place to work. This abdication of shared leadership cost us because no one was sharing information with us, listening to us, or guiding us through the processes that were impacting us as the crisis escalated. Part of shared leadership is showing up.

Academia is a hierarchy. Actually, all human organizations are hierarchical: think of governments, hospitals, or religious organizations. Even families are hierarchical. Take a look at the organizational chart of your institution. It is probably shaped like a pyramid. When I look at our university's organizational chart, I see the President at the top of the chart, layers of Assistant Vice Presidents below, deans and associate deans below that, and then departments. On the stage at convocation, where we sit for hours under bright lights watching happy students cross the stage, people who rank at the level of associate dean and higher have a water bottle placed at their seat. Department chairs on down do not.

While power can be exploited by people who are either ill-intentioned or oblivious, power is not inherently problematic. Martin Luther King Jr. told us that "Power properly understood is nothing but the ability to achieve purpose." He went on to say that "Power at its best is love implementing the demands of justice, and justice at its best is power correcting everything that stands against love" (King, 1967, p. 37). Power isn't evil.

There are clear advantages to working with people who have some amount of power. When a student works with an instructor or faculty supervisor, they benefit from expertise, and they receive mentorship. They benefit from the academic network the faculty member is able to introduce. Beyond the subject matter, supervisors have experience with management, publishing, grant writing, and professional progress. Allying with someone who has power is allying with someone who has the ability to achieve their goals. We all need to do that at some points in our careers.

People who are in leadership roles usually do not intentionally exploit their power to cause harm. In fact, leaders tend to want to care for and promote those who are in their charge (Haidt & Graham, 2007). That said, there is also evidence that people who have relatively more power may have a hard time understanding what is going on in the minds of those who have less power. It's not just that those at the top of the hierarchy are busy and are dealing with a wide variety of decisions and challenges. It is actually easier for a person who is lower in the hierarchy to infer what is happening in the minds of the higher-ups than vice versa.

Years ago, I conducted an experiment that showed that people with less power understand what is going on in other people's minds both more quickly and more accurately than people with more power. I experimentally created a power imbalance by randomly assigning people to be a "Winner" and "Loser" in a dyad. The Winner bested the Loser in a general knowledge competition that was rigged: the Winner had the easier set of questions. Then the Winner taught the Loser the sign language alphabet and critiqued them. Finally, the Loser had to solve puzzles while the Winner held the answer key and graded their performance. Subsequently, I measured how good each of these people were at inferring what was going on in others' minds. The Losers outperformed the Winners on these mind-reading tasks (Rutherford, 2004).

We put a great deal of effort into understanding, or guessing, what is in the minds of those whose power impacts us. We put less effort into understanding those who don't have enough power to impede our goals. Listening is part of the work of leadership, and it really is work. We have to be deliberate and intentional in order to understand those who report to us. If we leave it to chance, we will not understand. In order to influence the upper administration, we needed to help them to understand us, and if possible, collaborate with them.

Managing Up: Rebuilding Relationship Through Institutional Engagement

Just as the negative press began swirling, the university got a new provost. She arrived from another university. It was only three weeks after her arrival that the president of the university announced that our department's culture would be investigated. She had never met any of us, had never set foot in our building, and had never had the opportunity to get to know us and our good work, so she was vulnerable to being influenced by the story that was blowing up very publicly.

We needed the support of the provost, but it was too easy for her to believe that where there was smoke, there was surely some fire. Our reputation had been damaged not just in the eyes of the public, but in the eyes of our own administration.

Our department tried to "manage up." We were one of the most lucrative departments on campus because we taught so many students. Before the events of 2020, we had the reputation of being creative and productive in our research endeavors. We wanted the provost and other senior leaders to witness our contributions firsthand. We wanted to reframe their perceptions of us. By opening our doors, sharing our work, and showing up with professionalism and pride, we began to shift the narrative from suspicion to support.

There were two reasons we wanted our bosses in the upper administration to understand that we were a successful department. First, it felt bad not to be seen for who we are. We wanted the bosses to be proud of our contribution to the university. Second, we needed them to invest in rebuilding our department, and they were loath to do so as long as they saw us as a department full of bad characters. We needed a plan to "manage up" as a department. We had to build our reputation on campus, including with the provost.

After we had licked our wounds for a couple of years, our grievances against the university were settled, and The Flaherty investigation was underway, we could focus more effort into trying to help the university's administration see us in a positive light. We invited the provost to visit our building for the first time and to tour our research labs.

As you can imagine, it took weeks for her executive assistant to fit us into her schedule, but the provost walked over to see us on a cool day in April 2024. The stakes were high. I was not regarded highly by the university's administration, but I was still the chair, so I needed to represent the department, and we needed to improve our reputation. When she arrived, I greeted her at the door and took her coat, keeping it in my office during her visit. She spent two hours in the building and visited four different labs. Faculty and student researchers showed her some impressive research equipment and explained the basics of some of the experiments that were being conducted in our department.

We had never done anything like that before, opening up our labs to the provost, but it was important to us that the provost start to think of us in terms of the contribution that we were making to the university and stop thinking of us as a group of troublemakers. We needed her support.

Strategic Presence: Cultivating Influence Through Shared Governance

As a transgender leader, I thought I had much to offer, both in terms of lived experience and in terms of serving as a role model for others who might consider stepping into leadership. I spent a great deal of my time networking, but I needed to do more. I am only one person, and I have limited capacity for influence. By developing and supporting my colleagues, our department could expand its influence across the university. Over my five-year term, my colleagues got used to me asking them to "Keep showing up."

My departmental colleagues were on board with the idea of getting more involved in the governance of the university. We wrote in our five-year strategic plan "Across the university our reputation and relationships have been stained and strained by the negative publicity of 2020–2021. ... Both faculty and staff have reported that relationships with people in other units have turned chilly. It is in the best interest of the department to have constructive connections across the university. To this end, we will look to increase our presence across campus and temper our conflict with the Administration."

I encouraged faculty and students in my department to participate in university governance, run for office, pay attention to awards applications, and to network. I encouraged people to serve on selection committees for important positions and to join committees where we would have access to information and gain insight into how decisions were made. I encouraged people to network informally. We have been remarkably successful. During my time as chair, we have had a department member appointed to a position in the upper administration, four members who have served on the university senate, a department member who serves on the university planning committee, one on the board of governors, and one member served as president of our faculty association. Recently a colleague got appointed to the budget committee, a group whose meetings are always closed-door. Now we'll get a sense of how the sausage is made.

When I agreed to become the chair of the department, I was doing my dean a big favor and that was not the last time I offered to help the leaders of the university. A year and a half into my term as chair, the university started a search for someone to serve as vice president of DEI. I knew that the university would benefit from strong leadership in this domain, and they had just completed a review of the DEI office that resulted in some actionable advice. As a faculty member with lived experience as a transman and a lot of connections across the university, I thought I could be of help in this role. I wrote to the president and the provost of the university and told them I wanted to help them. They responded that I was welcome to apply for the position, which I did.

Early in my term as chair, I got an email from our faculty association asking for nominations for people to represent them on the university's sexual violence task force. Having representation on this committee would be important because the discrimination and harassment policy and the sexual violence policy were being revised. My predecessor would be ideal for this position. He had academic expertise that was relevant to the handling of such cases. He also had personal experience as the leader of our department when a number of such cases were in the news. I nominated him, the faculty association selected him, and for the next three years he represented our faculty association on this committee.

One of my colleagues was elected vice president of our faculty association and subsequently became president. In a university with a collegial governance system, the president of the faculty association is in a position to have a lot of influence. The president has a monthly meeting with the provost and deputy provost and also meets one-on-one with both the president and the provost. It was good for our department to be at the table with these people. We needed their help and support.

Fortuitously, this member of our department was serving as president of the faculty association when the university received the Flaherty Report in the summer of 2024. Because the investigation was a joint venture between the faculty association and the upper administration, he was able to receive the report in its entirety and publish a document summarizing the lessons learned. Had he not been in this position, the report might have gone into a file drawer, and the recommendations may not have been widely known.

When there was a rare opportunity to apply for a position in the upper administration, I supported the nomination of a colleague that I thought could represent our department well. His appointment has been entirely successful. He has had conversations with both the president and the provost and has been able to communicate with them about how our department is planning to repair and even what supports we would benefit from. He told them that I was providing strong leadership and trying to build a bridge with the administration. Without someone in the upper administration, it would have been very difficult to get the ear of the president and the provost. This new opportunity for advocacy has been impactful.

Several of my colleagues answered my invitation to run for the university senate and were elected. One of these colleagues discovered some procedural irregularities involving new policies being passed without proper review, policies that directly impacted the events of 2020. The issues were brought to the senate floor, and members of the senate were surprised that they had approved a policy that they had not had an opportunity to vet. The policy was reverted to its earlier version so that the senate could take time to read and consider the change. This colleague's work in the senate has been tremendously impactful.

One of the most important committees at the university is the university planning committee. It is not directly involved in governance the way the senate and the board of governors are, but it is involved in visioning and planning and therefore has access to loads of information. At their meetings, they discuss the most timely and relevant issues that the university is dealing with. I really wanted to have a member of my department on this committee. When the email came that there was an opening on this committee, I looked at my roster. Some of our most senior people were serving in important and time-consuming roles. I asked our most junior faculty member to consider serving on this committee. This was a person who is very smart and very savvy. Normally, I would not ask someone so junior because junior faculty members need to focus on their own productivity in preparation for a tenure review, but this person seemed to have the capacity for engaging in governance. They agreed to run and got elected. This placement was a success from the beginning. Despite being very junior, my colleague spoke up at meetings, asking relevant and sometimes cutting questions. Before long, I got an email from the provost telling me how impressed she was with my young colleague.

It was another of our newest faculty members who stepped up to run for the board of governors. She was untenured and too junior to vote against the rest of the body, but it was helpful having her in the room and reporting back to us what was going on in that very powerful body.

Our department increased visibility by participating in shared leadership as a deliberate strategy—placing colleagues in key governance roles, developing channels of communication, and building relationships across the university. Through our commitment to "keep showing up," we transformed marginalization into collaboration. With ears everywhere, our colleagues were able to keep our department in the loop. Choosing people in our group to represent us in the larger conversation had multiple advantages. First, we were in the right place to influence decisions and governance. Second, we had a representative who heard what was happening in the organization and could keep our group informed. Third, collaborating with the upper administration and people in power throughout the university helped us to gradually build trust and relationships, which was vital to allowing us to get our job done.

There are numerous opportunities to be involved in shared leadership across our university—opportunities for us to keep showing up, increase our visibility, increase our influence, and stay in the loop. Many of these happen on an annual cycle, like openings in the university's senate and the university's board of governors. I marked such opportunities in my calendar. Other announcements came out unexpectedly, so I kept an eye out for those as well. I passed these opportunities to our whole department in case there was someone who would be interested that I hadn't thought of. If no one stepped up, I reached out and issued an individual invitation to someone I thought was well suited for the role.

I tried to keep an eye on impact, making sure to have people in impactful positions where the important decisions are made. I tried to be strategic about putting people in the most impactful roles. For example, was the role primarily an opportunity to listen, or did I need to send someone who would be a strong advocate?

Celebrating Our Excellence: Visibility, Identity, and Renewal

In the aftermath of the demise of our reputation, our department reclaimed its identity through visibility. We strategically amplified our values, achievements, and community. These were designed not only to rebuild trust and recognition across campus but also to repair our own self-image. My colleagues and I tried to raise the profile of our department, employing several strategies over time.

In my first few months as chair, I organized a "Queer faculty reception." I had a poster designed that said, "The university's first transgender department chair invites you to the Queer Faculty Welcome Reception." I circulated the poster to all of the department chairs on campus and asked them to make the invitation available to faculty members in their department. I had the reception catered, and about 20 people attended. It was the first time on campus that there had been an event for all of the queer faculty, and it was a nice chance to meet people from across the disciplines. For me, it was not just a service, but some good networking. I was better able to understand who my allies were across campus. The fact that it was held in our department and hosted by the chair raised the profile of our department. Some people visited our building for the first time. These faculty members could see that they were welcome here. We were building bridges.

In the first few months of my being chair, our department created accounts on social media and started adding content. We announced publications, scientific talks, and departmental events. We announced hires and retirements, and of course we highlighted awards that department members won.

Later, in the spring of 2023, our department's associate chair of research started organizing a series of stories about our department for publication in the campus newspaper. She shared a document across the department so that people could sign up for a specific month and tell a story about the work they were doing. People contributed stories about research they were publishing and about community events. One story was about our department hosting a nationwide "Brain Bee," a competition for psychology students. One story reported that a department member had been appointed Officer of the Order of Canada, and another member had been elected Fellow of the Royal Society of Canada. There was a story about an undergraduate student who worked as a teaching assistant to other undergraduate students. A story ran about a student who was graduating, featuring both her research and her approach to parenting while being a full-time graduate student. For an entire year, a story about our department appeared in the campus paper every month. We were determined to share our good news.

Building Trust by Being There

Being involved in governance helped diminish the negative reputational consequences to our department, but we also needed to build relationships and trust. Trust is the foundation of leadership, and to succeed as a leader, you need to build trust with the people you lead. This goes both ways. A successful leader also needs to build a trusting relationship with those above, as well as the broader community. Collaborating on a project toward a shared goal is an effective way to rebuild trust. Trust is easy to break but takes years and multiple encounters to rebuild.

When I became chair, trust between the department and the upper administration had suffered. They did not trust us—they suspected us of harboring inappropriate behavior—and we no longer trusted them to protect and support us. When I sent my back-to-school email nine weeks into my term as chair, I needed The Supervisor to trust me to know what my department needed. She did not. I desperately needed to create trust so that I could get my job done.

In my fourth year of my five-year term, The Supervisor went on a leave, and I was reporting to an interim leader. He later shared with me that he had been warned about how difficult it would be to deal with our department, so I imagine he was expecting trouble when he first met with me. During our first meeting, we were both determined to not screw up this relationship. Although it was only an hour-long meeting, we spent an entire 15 minutes exchanging small talk before we got to business. We each talked about our kids and what they were up to in school. I told him where I shopped for shoes. He told me where he shopped for clothes. It was clear to me that we were both taking the time to invest in this relationship because we were not going to let it derail. This fifteen-minute chat was so different from any conversation I had had with The Supervisor. I always went to her supervisory meetings with a knot in my stomach. It was such a relief to have a supervisor that I could talk to, get feedback from, run ideas by, and ask questions of.

One strategy I employed to build trust was to network with people who were new in the university. I welcomed our Library's new diversity, equity, inclusion, and accessibility strategist, the university's new chaplain, our new associate dean of graduate studies, and our new associate dean academic. Networking with people is always valuable, and I've found that reaching out to new people is ideal: They appreciate the welcome, and they don't yet have a packed calendar.

In my first year as chair, my department sponsored a workshop for members of our university senate. Two of our department members who were serving on the university senate researched the history of collegial governance at our university. They gave a presentation and led a conversation. The department hosted the event and had it catered. Every senator on campus was invited. We were convinced that if the university had been following the processes of collegial governance that served as its foundation, our department would have had access to information and two-way communication as the events of 2020 were unfolding.

In addition to showing up for shared leadership at all levels of university governance, I encouraged my colleagues to show up for informal and social events as well. Every year, the president and vice presidents invite the entire campus to an ice cream social. I always attend this event and I bring all the department colleagues I can find to go with me. The president also has a barbecue picnic that kicks off the year. One year I went with a large group of my colleagues, all wearing T-shirts with our department's name and logo. We made sure to say "Hi" to the president.

One of my colleagues bought a lunch with the president at the annual United Way auction and invited a few of us to come along. This lunch never happened—we were told that the president had conflicts in his schedule—but we continued to accept every networking opportunity that came our way.

Our department cultivated relationships through governance, networking, and consistent visibility. By showing up in both formal and social spaces, we reestablished credibility, fostered mutual respect, and learned that trust is built conversation by conversation.

Awards and Celebrations

One strategy we used to repair our reputation was to nominate people for awards. Our department used award nominations as a strategic tool to spotlight excellence, rebuild credibility, and retell our story on our own terms. In 2024, I nominated one of my colleagues for the President's Award for Outstanding Teaching and Learning. Her teaching had already been recognized by the Student Union and the province-wide University Student Alliance. In her nomination, I described how she had created exciting and engaging experiential learning and used that engagement to sneak in content like math and neuroanatomy. When COVID-19 related restrictions made it impossible to import the crayfish that she used in her neuroscience laboratory course, she pulled on her waders and went into the local creek to find an alternative. I extolled her devotion to student education.

As a result of her winning the president's award, she and I were both invited to have lunch with the president of the university. The lunch took place in the alumni hall, a grand old building on campus. Ours was a small group, about 10 people, and the lunch itself took place in a small room, where we assumed that it would be impossible to avoid the highest-ranking members of the university administration, the hosts of the lunch. We were wrong.

When we arrived, there were assigned seats. My colleague, the award winner, was next to the president, and I was between her and a staff person. I enjoyed my lunch, chatting with my two seatmates. But my award-winning colleague had only me to talk to because the president managed to avoid saying a single word to her or even turning toward her during the meal. Our lunch with the president did not turn out to be the networking gold mine we had hoped for, but at the end of the lunch on his way out the door, the president stopped in his tracks, turned around, and said goodbye to me. The event was inherently socially awkward for us, and an example of our determination to "keep showing up" because we had the opportunity to raise the profile of the department.

Another colleague was elected to become a Fellow of the Royal Society of Canada. This colleague is one of our research superstars and has already held a number of prestigious awards. When he won, we hosted a day of talks delivered by his former students and held a big party. Of course, we invited the dean and the provost to this celebration.

Twice, I nominated a graduate student for the Governor General's Academic Medal, one of Canada's most prestigious awards given to students. She won in the fall of 2023, and the award was presented to her at commencement, an event attended by thousands including the president, the provost, the chancellor, and the dean.

We celebrate not just faculty and students, but also staff. In the last year of her 24 years in our department, we nominated our department manager for the President's Award for Outstanding Service. Former chairs and associate chairs provided nomination letters, remarking on her compassion, competence, and dedication to our department community. One nomination letter was signed by the 12 staff members who reported to her. We didn't win this award, but it was still an opportunity to raise the profile of the department.

Every year, I have nominated a faculty member from my department for the Outstanding Service Award organized by our faculty association. I have identified people who have made remarkable contributions to service, looked over their service record for their entire career, and written an application describing their service to the department, to the university, to creating research spaces, and to developing curriculum. Every year since I became chair, a member of our department has won.

In my fourth year, I nominated my predecessor. I had asked him the previous year if I could nominate him, but he had declined. He is a bit modest when it comes to being in the spotlight. This time around, I didn't ask him, I just put my nomination in. On the day of the awards ceremony, I was able to read a prepared speech describing why he deserved this award. The ceremony took place in the great hall of the same building where my colleague and I had lunched with the president. The great hall has the vaulted ceiling you see in British academic institutions, along with shields and insignias. It was a very serious place to receive an award. I described the care he took when leading our department to the assembled audience, which included his wife. I invited the audience to imagine what it would be like to lead the department while misinformation was swirling in the media, or when classes and graduate supervisory committees needed to be re-staffed in the middle of a term. I told him we were grateful for his "calm and thoughtful leadership." It was an opportunity to retell the story; this time from our point of view.

By honoring faculty, students, and staff through public ceremonies and private moments, we reclaimed our story and transformed recognition into repair.

The Quiet Work of Showing Up

As chair, I was encouraging my colleagues to keep showing up. I was nominating people in my department to leadership roles across the university and at the highest levels of university governance. While I was encouraging my colleagues to keep showing up, I challenged myself to do the same.

I have always been a quiet person. I'm an introvert and I never take up much space at a meeting. When I go to conferences, I have to remind myself that one of the functions of conferences is networking. I often do some work ahead of a conference to plan who I want to connect with. When I was an undergraduate at Yale, I made a commitment to myself that I would do something social every week. While some of my classmates were socializing from dawn until dusk and then some, I was deliberately planning to ask someone for lunch or for coffee once a week. When I got a faculty position, I similarly decided to reach out to a different colleague in my department every week for a lunch date. After a few weeks, I found that it felt too socially awkward, and I wasn't able to keep this practice up. I didn't understand how many of my colleagues seemed to find each other at lunch time on a regular basis. Mostly, I worked alone in my office.

When I became department chair, my responsibilities were different, and I was fully invested in doing a good job as leader and as an advocate for my department. As scrutiny increased, Human Resources was being called in to my supervisory meetings to document any missteps, and I was being pressured to leave my role as chair. I wanted to hide. I would have preferred to retreat to my office and close the door. But I had to find the courage to keep showing up to events across campus. I had made a commitment to my department, and I was going to continue to do my best.

I continued to accept invitations to campus-wide events. I attended talks organized by my colleague who is an Associate Vice President working in the area of society and impact. I continued to attend leadership development workshops. I enrolled in a mental health workshop for university leaders. I attended a "speed networking" event sponsored by the Associate Vice President of Research where I spent three minutes each with a number of colleagues across campus talking about our research programs. I networked with student leaders on campus. Three and a half years into my term, I received an invitation to the holiday mixer sponsored by The Administrator. This was after she had hired a law firm and organized a secret report to help build her case for removing me from my role as chair. I was still chair of the department and I wanted to represent our department well, so I accepted the invitation. I wore a garish holiday tie.

References

Brown, B. (2006). Shame resilience theory: A grounded theory study on women and shame. *Families in Society: The Journal of Contemporary Social Services, 87*, 43–52. https://doi.org/10.1606/1044-3894.3483

Ferguson, T. J., Eyre, H. L., & Ashbaker, M. (2000). Unwanted identities: A key variable in shame-anger links and gender differences in shame. *Sex Roles, 42*, 133–157. https://doi.org/10.1023/A:1007061505251

Haidt, J., & Graham, J. (2007). When morality opposes justice: Conservatives have moral intuitions that liberals may not recognize. *Social Justice Research, 20*(1), 98–116.

King, M.L. (1967). *Where do we go from here.* 11th Annual Convention of the Southern Christian Leadership Conference (pp. 1–22). Southern Christian Leadership Conference.

Munt, S. (2008). *Queer attachments: The cultural politics of shame.* Ashgate Publishing Ltd.

Rutherford, M. D. (2004). The effect of social role on theory of mind reasoning. *British Journal of Psychology, 95*(1), 91–103. https://doi.org/10.1348/000712604322779488

Scheff, T. J. (2003). Shame in self and society. *Symbolic Interaction, 26*, 239–262. https://doi.org/10.1525/si.2003.26.2.239

Silfver, M. (2007). Coping with guilt and shame: A narrative approach. *Journal of Moral Education, 36*, 169–183. https://doi.org/10.1080/03057240701325274

Torres, W. J., & Bergner, R. M. (2010). Humiliation: Its nature and consequences. *Journal of the American Academy of Psychiatry and the Law, 38*(2), 195–204.

9

Please Don't Destroy: Compassion in Accountability

A persistent challenge for leaders is responding to demands for accountability. When you find yourself in a leadership role, people will show up at your door and ask you to hold someone accountable for something they have done or said that offended somebody. As I stepped into a leadership position, I had a close-up view of the impact that resulted when leaders fumble their attempts at holding someone accountable. Our department had been publicly accused of "complacency that has let inappropriate behaviors go unchecked." My department had been dumped by the cancel culture. We felt public humiliation. I knew I needed to develop my own approach to accountability, and I was determined to bring compassion to the task.

Holding someone accountable means requiring them to be responsible for their actions and words. If someone does or says something that creates harm, holding them accountable means expecting them to either redress the harm (maybe by apologizing and making reparations) or to justify their actions. In the workplace, it is usually the group's leader who is expected to hold someone to account, although sometimes the task gets passed to a human resources department.

Holding someone accountable protects the community. If we can guide people back to the community's standards of civility and care, then we protect the community from the erosion of those standards. A transgression of those expectations that is allowed to go unaddressed can have the effect of changing the community's expectations and ultimately the culture.

At times, I have been called on by members of my community to hold someone accountable, as when a student felt a professor had fallen short of their supervisory responsibilities. I have been called on by people external to our community to hold someone in my department accountable. Once I had a journalist email me and ask me to take a professor to task for not responding to an inquiry as helpfully as the journalist had wanted. In those cases, the person who approached me was angry and wanted me to extract the desired accountability.

Sometimes the request for accountability comes from above. My dean asked that I make sure that everyone in my department is working hard enough so that the university is getting its money's worth out of each faculty member. One time my supervisor presented me with an email that was written by a faculty member in my department. She asked me to read it and describe the tone. I said it sounded terse. She wanted me to hold the faculty member accountable for sending an email that sounded terse.

Twice I've had Human Resources reach out to me, instructing me to make someone behave more professionally or comply with a policy. In one case, I was asked to make sure faculty members in my department were complying with guidelines that had emerged during the COVID-related lockdowns. The guidelines said that people could not work while they were out of the province. This became problematic once people started traveling more because faculty and students in my department do field work in other provinces and other countries, they attend conferences, and they collaborate with scholars all over the world. In this case, a faculty member had left the province to attend a funeral. I was asked to tell her she was violating policy and hold her accountable. I clearly needed to develop a compassionate strategy to deal with these requests for accountability.

Building a Culture of Calling In

One constructive and inclusive approach to thinking about accountability comes from the work of Paula Cole Jones. Paula is a Management Consultant and Diversity Strategist who creates inclusive communities. She often works in faith communities. She visited my church just after we adopted our 8th principle, which she coauthored. Our 8th principle says that we:

> Covenant to affirm and promote: Individual and communal action that accountably dismantles racism and systemic barriers to full inclusion in ourselves and our institutions.

During her visit, a congregant asked how we were to understand and implement this call to accountability. Paula explained that this word "accountability" did not mean determining whether someone had done or said something that was "wrong." We were not to refer to some policy or external standard in order to determine whether someone should be punished. The accountability was to our covenant—our community's expectations about how we treat one another. Our obligation was to the relationship we have with one another. Accountability means using our expectations of our shared relationship to guide people back to the group covenant.

Importantly, the relationship has to precede the accountability. It is only by building the relationship that we have the opportunity to support the covenant. When this covenant is violated, we check in with one another. We make sure we have the common understanding we thought we had regarding how we treat each other and speak to each other. We talk about whether recent acts or words were consistent with our shared expectations. We may decide together that repair is necessary. If someone is out of covenant—they are behaving in a way that is contrary to the covenant the community holds—you can invite them to come back into covenant. They may need to apologize or offer reparations in order to do so.

This task of holding people accountable, of correcting behaviors that might have been inconsistent with our communal values, was new to me when I stepped into leadership. From my work in leadership in my church community, I was familiar with the concept of calling people into covenant—to request that people treat each other in the way that honored our covenant. But now my job required me to hold people to account, and I wanted to make sure that I didn't cause harm.

Just prior to my becoming chair, our department hosted Loretta Ross, a writer, scholar, and reproductive rights activist, as a colloquium speaker. We were intrigued by her criticism of the "call-out culture." Following that introduction, I have taken several workshops with her and Loan Tran, the activist-educator who coined the term "calling in" in contrast to "calling out," and I have embraced this approach in my leadership. This approach is both compassionate and effective.

According to Ross, if you shame someone, you are not fostering a situation where that person can learn, reflect, and think creatively about solutions going forward. If you humiliate someone, you'll put them in a defensive position, and it is unlikely that they will be able to critically examine their actions. And if you call them out publicly, you run the risk of ending the relationship. "When we call students out instead of building a call-in culture in the classroom, we contribute to increasingly toxic and polarized conversations. And we make learning less inviting" (Ross, 2019, p. 20). Like Paula Cole Jones, Ross emphasized that you will need to rely on a trusting relationship to engage someone in professional and personal development.

Calling in means inviting someone to reflect on shared values and consider whether their actions have been consistent with those values. Ross uses both quotidian and extreme examples. She describes talking to her uncle after an offensive comment made at the Thanksgiving dinner table. She told him that she knew he didn't want to hurt people and discussed with him alternatives to what he had said. At the other extreme, Ross tells the story of a man who had been convicted of rape who wrote to her saying he wanted to learn how not to be a rapist. Instead of lashing out in anger, she called him in, holding him accountable, doing so with the intention of helping him develop as a person. It was due to that experience that she was able to start articulating the idea of calling in. She went on to call in former KKK members.

When my department created our five-year strategic plan, we were familiar with Dr. Ross's teachings. We were stinging from being called out, and we didn't want to amplify that harm. We wanted to talk about creating a culture of calling in. We wrote in our strategic plan:

> When missteps happen, we call in, rather than call out (as we learned from Loretta Ross). Over the next five years, we will practice our Core Values, care for our community, learn new skills, and create a strong foundation so that people love being here.

By fostering trust and aligning with shared values, leaders can create inclusive cultures of learning and belonging.

Calling Out Hurts

Melanie and I applied these ideas in a workshop on "Radically Inclusive Leadership" that we delivered to a group of Unitarian Universalist leaders. We talked about calling out and calling in and walked through our step-by-step instructions for calling in. Then we asked the attendees if they had ever been called out. Nearly everyone raised their hand. Being called out is memorable; it is something that people will ruminate on for years to come.

After the workshop, a shy young leader came up to us and told us his story of being called out. It was during a discussion about trans folks, and he asked a question about the use of pronouns. He asked whether you were supposed to use the current or the former pronouns when telling a story about someone before they transitioned. In his mind, his question was constructive, and it came from a place of genuine innocence and curiosity. But the discussion leader called him out in front of the whole group. He was told that his question was harmful and transphobic. He was deeply ashamed by this calling out, and he removed himself from the group. In fact, he didn't engage with that group or any group for the next three years.

What I learned from this conversation was, when you are in a leadership role, you need to be mindful of the power that you have and the impact that your words have. The task of holding someone accountable is a tricky task that has the potential to do tremendous harm to individuals and to your community if done recklessly. This is true whether they are guilty of the offense they were accused of or not.

Melanie and I have led workshops on radically inclusive leadership, queer etiquette, queer parenting, and religion and queer values. We've led workshops on formal consensus decision-making several times. We have also been participants in many more workshops, including workshops on anti-racism and on breaking down categorical barriers in community. Years ago, we were downtown in a room in the local conventions center. The room was full of queer and trans people we knew, and the workshop was being facilitated by a local trans man that we had known for many years. The topic was organizing the community to advocate for trans health care, and attendees were invited to contribute to the discussion. A participant raised her hand and offered a comment about the "GLBTQ" community. The facilitator called her out. "We say 'LGBTQ' now in order to acknowledge that queer women are more oppressed than gay men." The participant felt called out in front of our community. It stung. For the rest of the workshop, she was more hesitant to contribute to the discussion. This is an example of a phenomenon Dr. Ross wants us to think about: those of us on the left police each other, insisting on the correct way to be correct. We'll call each other out instead of uniting in our mission.

Don't fall for the calling-out trap, even if it seems intuitively appealing. Even if someone you lead has done something that is offensive and has violated your covenant, this person is still under your care as a leader. Part of your job is to figure out how best to mentor them. Shame doesn't foster learning. Divisiveness doesn't foster learning. Be gentle in guiding your people to self-discovery and personal growth. Effective leadership prioritizes mentorship over punishment.

Calling In: Small and Large

One of the points that Dr. Ross makes in her book, *Calling In: How to Start Making Change with Those You'd Rather Cancel*, is that calling in may challenge your instincts. You may feel like lashing out and harming someone who has offended you. Or if you can restrain yourself from harming another person, you still may feel the impulse to silence them or remove them from your community. Calling in actually has the effect of further incorporating the offender into your community and bringing them closer to the values of the community (Ross, 2025).

Melanie and I had an opportunity to use our calling-in practice not too long ago at a large gathering of our recently found extended family. We had used anonymous donor sperm to grow our family, and when our kids were young, I discovered a group online of families who had used the same donor to make babies. My kids have dozens of half-siblings. Over the years, we spent time with this group of kids who look a lot like our kids and generally share a lot of interests. These kids have the easy relationship of found siblings.

During the era of COVID-related travel restrictions we had a few online gatherings. During one of those Zoom gatherings, we saw one of the half-siblings in his bedroom and could not help but notice the huge confederate flag on his bedroom wall. We didn't call him out online, but we had to say something. We waited until we were in person to talk to him about his flag.

We assumed good intent, and we assumed a bit of innocence, since he was only 16 years old at the time. We asked him about his flag. We asked him what it meant to him. He said for him it was a symbol of southern pride, a signal that he belonged in the south. We asked him what he thought the flag meant to other people. His innocence, I believe, was genuine. We told him that some people could be harmed by a display of the confederate flag. We gave him a bit of history.

We were explicit that we didn't think he would want to harm other people as we talked to him about the history of the flag and the impact it might have on other people who saw that he displayed the flag. The gap analysis was the comparison between his intended impact and his actual impact. He seemed surprised and not at all defensive as he considered his potential impact on people he cared about.

Listen Before Picking Sides

The first thing to remember when someone knocks on your door and asks for justice is that you are hearing one side of the story. If you were not in the room, you may be getting a skewed report. Effective leadership requires resisting reactive demands for discipline. Impulsive punishment will damage your relationship with those who trust you. In my recent experience, it is very difficult to rebuild this trust and repair a relationship once this type of blunder has been made.

At one point when I was department chair, I was contacted by the Ombudsman's office. This is an office that receives complaints from people who feel that they have been wronged or that they need help navigating a conflict. Often a student approaches the Ombudsman for help with a professor. In this case, the Ombudsman wanted to talk to me about a faculty member in my department. The faculty member had asked a student to drop a course when they were several weeks into the term and the student wasn't making any progress. The professor estimated that it was too late in the term to successfully complete the course. The student was offended, wanted more support, wanted it to be possible to complete the course, and told the Ombudsman as much. I was called to a meeting with the Ombudsman.

The Ombudsman wanted me to discipline the faculty member. She wanted me to charge them with a violation of the faculty code of conduct. She also wanted me to launch an investigation into the culture in this faculty member's lab. Although she hadn't spoken to the faculty member, to her it seemed clear that if this faculty member was so irresponsible for the care of one student, they must be treating other students just as poorly, and an investigation would surely reveal this systemic problem. To her, the correct thing to do was to dig in and find as much evidence as possible against this professor.

I had some practical questions about this investigation. First of all, who was going to pay for it? In my experience these investigations are expensive, and it wasn't in the department's budget. Second, once I gathered data from the laboratory in question (I imagine some students would say it's great, some students would say they don't get enough attention from their supervisor), what would I compare my findings to? In order to complete an interpretable investigation, I would need comparators. Third, how would I wrap up the investigation if I discovered there were no problems that were unique to this lab? I would need to have a plan for both the expected and the unexpected outcome.

But there were more fundamental leadership considerations. If I launched an investigation into this colleague's laboratory, would I ever have an opportunity to mentor them again? Knowing that trust and relationship are fundamental to leadership, should I break this trust in order to possibly find some incriminating evidence? How would I rebuild trust with the faculty member so that we could continue to work constructively together? If I launched an investigation in order to discipline my colleague, would I even get to have a constructive conversation about student supervision, or would our relationship be so damaged that I never got a mentorship opportunity?

At the same time, I didn't want to leave the student or the Ombudsman thinking that I didn't care about their concerns. I knew that the Ombudsman had not had a conversation with my colleague, but I thought it might be constructive for me to do so. I figured the story would be told differently from the other side, and I might learn something.

I invited my colleague to have a conversation. I was very transparent: I told him that I had been contacted by the Ombudsman. I told him that the student had initiated that communication. I showed him the policies that the Ombudsman wanted me to bring to his attention. We discussed what might have gone better and what might have been a misinterpretation on the part of the student or the Ombudsman. I trusted my colleague to listen and to consider his impact on the student and to reflect on anything that he wanted to do differently in the future. This conversation was more constructive than any investigation. We did not damage our relationship, and the student was able to complete the course with a different supervisor. By seeking understanding before judgment, leaders preserve relationships and foster a culture where accountability leads to dialogue not damage.

How to Call Someone In

I've learned, largely from Dr. Ross, that calling someone in is a deliberate and relational process rooted in shared values and psychological safety. Dr. Ross describes how to leverage relationships in order to create a safe environment where learning listening and perspective taking are possible. You meet the offending person where they are, engage their sympathy to your common goals, point to impact, and invite them to think about whether they want to do anything differently.

Calling someone in is going to work best if you base the conversation in common values or shared goals. If you are in a community or a department that has explicitly named its core values, you can refer to those values. You may be in a community that has a covenant or a policy on constructive communication, in which case you can refer to that. If not, you can always center your conversation on the mission and vision statement of your organization because these statements also name shared values.

Assume good intent and validate the individual as a person: "I know that you intended to be helpful," or "I know that you care a lot about our department," for example, could affirm one's intentions. Assume that they are trying to do something that they think is constructive and then see if you can understand what that is. They likely value the cohesiveness of the community. Check on that explicitly. They probably are trying to advance the mission of the university or the goals of the organization. Ask them explicitly if that is what they are doing. They very likely would prefer to avoid harming anyone. Again, ask them to make that explicit. Once they have clarified their values, goals and intentions, endorse them. Acknowledge that they have the intention of building up the community and supporting the mission of the organization.

Once you are on the same page about the values that underlie their actions, you can work through a gap analysis. Compare intention and impact. Compare the impact they intended to have to the impact they actually had. If you get them to reflect on the difference between their intended and actual impact, then you have an opportunity to ask whether they would do anything differently in the future. They'll need to feel safe with you in order to admit, even to themselves, that their words did not land as intended.

Help them brainstorm but let them lead the way. I have learned that even though I usually go into the meeting with a planned outcome, it is still useful to let the other person generate solutions. They will find their own suggestions more palatable, so it will be easier to get them to commit to the plan. And who knows, they may come up with better suggestions than you. When I met with my colleague who had sent a terse email, I thought I was going to offer a solution to this problem: pause before sending an angry email. Sleep on it and edit the email when emotions have subsided. My colleague came up with a completely different solution: ask an artificial intelligence program to make the message sound polite and professional. I hadn't thought of that.

I've found it useful to schedule plenty of time for these conversations. The person who has created a negative impact may want to rebut the accusation. Recently, a student reached out to me to complain that a faculty member's mentorship was inadequate. The faculty member brought "evidence" and wanted me to look at emails and documents that defended recent decisions. I made space for that. My colleagues were willing to listen to me, but only after I had listened to them. The gap analysis sometimes took more than one meeting. That's okay. I was investing in an individual's professional development as well as supporting my organization's commitment to its culture. By affirming intent, exploring the gap between impact and intention and collaborative solutions, leaders can transform moments of harm into opportunities for growth.

Part of the psychological safety that is required for reflection and growth is the possibility of forgiveness. It is painful to sit in a place of shame. When our department was accused of "complacency" that allowed inappropriate behavior, the administrations solution was a mandatory Zoom webinar for our department. We all attended. But nearly a year later, several of us heard that members of the administration still thought that our department had a problematic culture. We were floored. We thought that we were being offered a path to redemption with the webinar. We needed to be released from the doghouse. A calling-in conversation needs to offer a resolution.

Barack Obama has been vocal about his concerns about "cancel culture" since at least 2019. He stresses that the world is messy, and none of us are going to get it right all of the time, so there has to be some grace. We need to find ways to stay in relationship when mistakes are made. We have to have the capacity to forgive.

Finally, you need to close the communication loop. You need to get back to the person who originally brought the complaint to you. They need to hear clearly that you have taken their concerns seriously. You may not be able to deliver what they originally asked you for—to fire the offending employee, for example—but they need to hear that you have appreciated the gravity of the situation. They need to know that the community's covenant has been preserved. I always invite the complainant to stay in communication with me and let me know if things get better or if things get worse. If you don't loop back to the person who brought the concern to you, resentment may fester.

Explicit Goals Constrain Biases

Before I initiate a calling in conversation, I get clear on my goals for the encounter. My goal is almost always professional development or sometimes personal growth. I can then focus on the goal when designing my approach.

At one point, The Supervisor told me that I needed to put one of my employees on a Professional Improvement Plan, or what she called a PIP. She mentioned that sometimes when an employee is put on a PIP, they just leave the organization, and you don't have to work with them to improve. She listed a number of criticisms she had regarding this employee and I took notes. I said, "Okay, I'll have a talk with her about these concerns." The Supervisor retorted "No! This is all confidential!"

If I had concerns about an employee's performance, I would talk to them right away and see if we could find workable solutions. I would make sure we had shared expectations regarding their job and see if there was anything they needed from me to help them do their job. It would never occur to me to keep my concerns confidential. After that, I received two rounds of draft PIPs, each with a "Confidential" watermark. When the employee was finally called into a meeting, she was faced with a panel that included The Supervisor, two members of The Supervisor's staff, and Human Resources. I had not been allowed to share the concerns. I had noticed from my own experience that meetings with Human Resources seem to be organized to maximize surprise and prevent preparation. My employee was finally told what the concerns were. She left the department voluntarily.

When dealing with accountability, it is extremely important to be aware of cognitive biases. We are especially vulnerable to responding to our own biases and prejudices when meting out punishments. We know that, in the criminal justice system, race has an impact on the severity of punishment (Maratea, 2019) and rates of incarceration (Fellner et al., 1995), and we know that this difference is predicted by bias and prejudice (Cooley et al., 2019). Think about that before you call out someone who is depending on you for leadership and mentorship. Leaders must manage their own biases and design interventions that foster growth and preserved dignity, especially when power dynamics and personal feelings complicate the path forward. Take care before you discipline someone in your care.

Sometimes you will find it necessary to have difficult conversations with someone you don't have positive feelings toward. You can manage these conversations by keeping your goal in mind. Design your interventions so that you won't harm and alienate the person and so that learning and development are the most likely result. It will be particularly important that your message and any sanctions you choose are designed to develop that person. I've been impacted negatively when implicit biases allowed those who had power over me to stop thinking of me as a person. If the person you are engaging with is someone you dislike, be especially cautious. If you are about to engage in a process that is designed to harm someone, take a moment to reevaluate. Just because you have the power to create distress doesn't mean that's good leadership.

It is also worth asking whether your goal is performative. Barack Obama commented that some young activists think the surest way to make change is "to be as judgmental as possible about other people" (Obama, 2019, p. 29). We are living in a cultural moment when people are making attempts to increase their status by publicly calling people out. Sometimes it seems that there is a race to be the first to identify the use of out-of-date terminology or catch someone making an assumption. There is a name for this attempt at displaying how up-to-date our awareness is: virtue signaling.

Performative Advocacy

An awareness of transgender experiences and concerns is something that people may use to display their cultural competence, but there are times when I cringe at attempts to be supportive. Well-intentioned efforts to demonstrate allyship can backfire. Recently a cisgender person who I'm connected with on social media posted a news story about a trans man being brutally murdered. She declared her outrage. I went down the rabbit hole and read the details of the case, which were terrifying and disturbing. Obviously, she hadn't shared this story with me in mind. She was signaling to her network that she was empathetic toward transgender people.

There are a number of reasons to be cautious about speaking up on behalf of someone else's group. You might be speaking about something you don't quite understand, escalating a disagreement, or even putting someone in danger. When I was much younger, I worked as a forest firefighter on a crew. One day when we were deep in the forest, our crew encountered another fire crew. After some mingling and chatting, a firefighter from the other crew expressed the opinion that all gay people should be killed. A member of my crew yelled out, "Oh! Mel's gay!"

I knew my crewmate to be a liberal progressive who publicly advocated for gay rights and feminism. But as a straight person, he was not the right person to be speaking up about gay rights at that moment and certainly not the person to be making the perilous decision that I should be outed to homophobic strangers in the forest. Maybe he thought he was being helpful. Maybe he was showing me that I was okay with him, even if this other firefighter thought I should be killed. I wished that we were not deep in the woods.

Obviously, there are cultural advantages to a community where people choose their words thoughtfully so as not to cause harm or offense. But are you the right person to be holding someone accountable for their word choice? Is the person you are speaking with the right person to be holding to account? In my lab, we do research having to do with the impact of social category membership on how people are perceived. Recently, we have been looking at religious identity as a social category. A student of mine who is Muslim traveled to a conference to present her research finding that mental representations of Christian faces are rated more positively than mental representations of Muslim faces. It happened to be her first conference, and her first time presenting her research outside of our lab.

A middle-aged white man, someone who was rather well established in his career, came to her poster and expressed how angry it made him that our research examines the perception of Muslim people. He had a strong sense that there must be something racist in our assumption that these topics could be studied. A middle-aged white professor was lecturing a young Muslim student about Islamophobia. She was quite shaken.

She and I then submitted our research for publication, reporting that participants in our lab had distinct visual perceptions of Christian and Muslim faces. The editor asked us to remove the words Christian and Muslim. So, we resubmitted the paper, referring to "Group A" and "Group B." This utterly confused the reviewers who asked us to tell them who these groups were. What was the point of this research? We reinstated the categorical labels and were then told that the paper would be published. Months later we learned that the editor had subsequently run the paper by their DEI committee, who said that it could not be published with the religious labels. We eventually got this all sorted out, and the paper was published with a group of people who self-identified as Christian labeled "Christian" and a group of people who self-identified as Muslim labeled "Muslim." Are you sure that you are the right person to be holding someone accountable?

Accountability requires humility, discernment, and a deep understanding of whether it is for you to speak. Before you confront someone for using what you think are the wrong words, make sure that it is your place. Perhaps it is, but do the work of considering whether you understand the nuance. Before calling someone out publicly, examine your motives. Could the conversation happen in private? Would that lead to a satisfactory outcome, even if you don't get the glory publicly? Maybe it's not about you.

The Ripple Effect of Trust and Curiosity

Recently a student of mine called me in. This was a student who is doing work in my lab and who had taken my "Evidence-Based Equity, Diversity and Inclusion" course. We were working on a paper she had written, and I noticed what I thought was an odd turn of phrase. I asked, "Is English your first language?" She and I had a deep and trusting relationship, and she was able to point out the impact that this question could have. I was literally othering her—making a categorical distinction between her and students in my lab who were native speakers of English. While editing her paper, I could have just offered a phrase that sounded clearer to me without querying her linguistic background. I was impressed with her skill at calling me in. I acknowledged her observation about my question, and I apologized. I haven't made the same mistake again because she called me back into covenant. It is especially impressive that she was able to call me in, given that I am her supervisor. Even hierarchical relationships can become spaces for learning and reflection.

Once I began practicing calling in as the leader of the department and once calling in became not just part of our vocabulary but an expectation, I could see how deeply this expectation impacted our department's culture. I saw it clearly one day when a number of professors came to talk to me about a staff person who they didn't think was working to potential. From the very beginning of the meeting, they made it clear that they wanted me to approach this staff member with curiosity. They wanted me to start my conversation with the staff person by checking in to see if they were okay, and only then to inquire whether there was anything the staff person might need to better fulfill their duties. Perhaps they needed more clarity about expectations. These professors wanted me to approach the staff person with compassion while working toward a more effective execution of their job. This meeting took place about 3 and a half years into my term as chair. I was struck by how clear these concerned faculty members were that we should have a compassionate and constructive meeting, without relaxing our expectation of excellent work. I felt so satisfied that this call to accountability was full of compassion, without one hint of calling out.

If you leverage a trusting relationship, you have created a safe space where someone you supervise does not feel defensive and you'll often find success in this method. Even when you don't get to the destination you intended, you have likely made some progress. It is possible that your employee will go on to think about what you talked about and will draw some constructive conclusions following the conversation. As calling in became part of our department's culture, it fostered not only accountability but mutual growth.

It is possible that creating the calling-in culture will impact everyone in your organization, including you. Following a conversation in which you call someone in, the conversation might stick with you. Perhaps you will walk away with a deeper understanding of the circumstances that led to the behavior at issue. This might ultimately lead you to be more forgiving, or it might lead you to examine the systemic issues in your organization that contributed to the behavior. The professional development that results may be your own.

When Calling In Is Not the Right Tool

Calling in has limits. While calling in can foster growth and repair, it is not always safe, feasible, or effective. You may find someone too resistant to engage in the conversation you want to have. You may not have established a strong enough relationship to create the psychological safety necessary to call someone in. You may not wish to be in a relationship with a specific person as might happen when you have been harmed by a stranger and find it easier to keep on walking. If someone intends harm, then calling in will not be effective.

It is also possible that you don't have the time or the emotional capacity to save the world today. If you are the person who has been harmed, you may find it hard to invest the emotional labor in someone's personal growth. You may find that you are too personally vulnerable to be the one to call someone in. You don't have to. It may be necessary to protect yourself and that is totally fair. Take care of yourself.

You may not be able to call someone in because they have power over you. I have found it extremely challenging to call in people who have power over me, either when they are harming me or when they are harming others. When The Supervisor and The Administrator were having a series of disciplinary meetings with me, they were not curious about my perspective, and attempts to have conversations with them were not only futile, but dangerous. Every conversation was documented with the intention of finding evidence to support a case for removing me. I found no opportunities for calling in.

When I asked for a meeting with the provost and the president just prior to becoming chair, I did not get the sense that they were understanding the impact their actions had had on my department. The provost appeared to be texting while we met over Zoom. The president followed the meeting with an email saying how "disappointed" he and the provost were with me during the meeting. Calling in wasn't working.

Loretta Ross, whose expertise on calling in and calling out I value deeply, believes that calling out is sometimes the most effective way to hold someone to account. The correct circumstance for calling out is almost always when a person with little power is trying to hold someone with great power to account. Ross says, "Call outs are most effective when they target powerful people beyond our reach and when public scrutiny is a strategic weapon we deploy against the unreachably powerful" (Ross, 2025, p. 42). Calling out is sometimes our only option when there is a great power disparity and "When trust and good faith have already been exhausted" (Ross, 2025, p. 44).

After The Supervisor swore and raised her middle finger to me, I filed a claim because I did not feel safe at work. I was not going to be able to develop our relationship by working directly with The Supervisor. When The Administrator responded to my claim with a "single incident involving inappropriate language does not always constitute a violation of the Human Rights Code" and told me I was "not to circumvent or avoid communication with [The Supervisor]," I needed help. The Administrator was so high ranking that there was no help for me at the university. I sought help at the Human Rights Tribunal of Ontario by filing a human rights application. Later, when The Administrator hired an outside law firm to investigate me, I updated my human rights claim to include her further actions. I was disappointed there was not a more collaborative path to creating a working relationship. I went into the role deeply believing that I had the skills to work through conflicts by orienting the conversation to shared values. I was unable to make this approach work across a great power imbalance. Self-protection and strategic calling out may be necessary tools for accountability, particularly when institutional structures are barriers to safety.

Through my network of transgender allies, I learned there is little case law for transgender employees. Employers settle disputes by exchanging cash for a non-disclosure agreement which means that stories don't get told and decisions don't set precedent.

By prioritizing compassion over performative discipline, leaders create the psychological safety necessary for meaningful change and develop a culture of inclusion. Our department's strategic five-year plan points to our commitment to repairing our relationships and mentions our intention to call people in, when necessary. In my time as chair, I never regretted prioritizing compassion.

References

Cooley, E., Lei, R., Brown-Iannuzzi, J., & Ellerkamp, T. (2019). Personal prejudice, other guilt: Explicit prejudice toward Black people predicts guilty verdicts for White officers who kill Black men. *Personality and Social Psychology Bulletin, 45*(5), 754–766. https://doi.org/10.1177/0146167218796787

Fellner, J., Walsh, N., Roth, K., & Smart, J. (1995). *Punishment and prejudice: Racial disparities in the war on drugs.* Human Rights Watch.

Maratea, R. J. (2019). *Killing with prejudice: Institutionalized racism in American capital punishment.* NYU Press.

Obama, B. (2019). *Remarks at the Obama foundation summit.* Obama Foundation. https://www.obama.org

Ross, L. J. (2019). Speaking up without tearing down. *Teaching Tolerance, 61,* 19–22. https://www.learningforjustice.org/magazine/spring-2019/speaking-up-without-tearing-down?utm-medium=email&utm_source=Teaching+Tolerance&utm_campaign=dae829210c-Newletter+2-27-2019&utm_medium=email&utm_term=028cea207c3-dae829210c-&utm_term=0_a8cea027c3-06fdf59172-83006303

Ross, L. J. (2025). *Calling In: How to start making change with those you'd rather cancel.* Simon and Schuster.

10

Lessons Learned: The Exit Interview I Gave Myself

My term as chair was quite literally a test of my faith. I started my term with a core belief in my ability to connect with people so that we could mutually create both solutions and relationships. That belief was put to the test. More fundamentally, my leadership was rooted in my values, and my very approach to leadership was tested.

Despite the barriers and setbacks, my journey has reaffirmed my conviction that leadership is a radical act of care. It is about holding space for voices too often silenced and standing firm when the cost is high. Leadership requires more than symbolic gestures or compliance checklists. It requires an ongoing commitment to listening deeply, embracing complexity, and fostering trust across diverse communities.

As a transgender man, I was able to step into a Glass Cliff leadership position. As I led my department through its crisis, I learned a lot about how to lead successfully in troubled times. As my term wrapped up, I took the time to reflect. This is what I learned from the exit interview I gave myself.

Values Are Your Compass

The more complex and challenging the leadership situation, the more you'll need to be guided by your values.

Organizations need to explicitly define their values and mission. Failing to name your values means things will be harder when challenging situations come along. On a good day, a leader who hasn't identified their guiding values might get along fine by relying on the historical direction of the organization. In a time of crisis, you will be lost if you don't know what values underpin your decisions and your leadership. In moments of organizational turmoil, clearly defined values and mission are essential.

Given how successful I felt bringing value-based governance to my department, I was confused when The Administrator tried to remove me from my position. In my first meeting with The Administrator and Human Resources, I explained that I was taking a values-based approach to leadership and that I was prioritizing integrity and compassion. When The Administrator wanted me to step down, I considered it. I told her that I would do so if I thought it was in the best interest of the department. She seemed energized by this answer. I really meant it, and it continued to be true throughout my term: I would step down if doing so served my department.

When The Administrator told me that "the status quo could not continue," I decided to hold fast to my commitment to my department because I believed our shared values were serving my department. I never thought that my resignation was best for my department—for a couple of reasons: First, I thought the continuity in leadership had value. Second, there was no one else in the department who was interested in the job. When The Administrator indicated that our next chair could be someone from outside of our department, I didn't think that was prudent because someone unfamiliar with what had happened in our traumatized department might not have brought the required care to the position. I remained firm. It was intimidating, yes, but I refused to allow her to pressure me into breaking my commitment. My values allowed me to guide my department, even in the face of institutional pressure.

Have a Development Mindset

Use your position in leadership to support the professional development of your people.

I mentored the department's associate chairs on a series of leadership topics when we met quarterly. I made sure most of the department had an opportunity to participate in the annual evaluation committee so that everyone understood that process. I met monthly with our newest faculty members to make sure they were prepared for tenure and promotion. I was investing in my people and developing succession options.

Leadership is not a solo journey but a collective endeavor, and you can take steps to develop leaders on your team. Lots of types of people are appropriate for leadership, and not all leadership skills are self-evident. By recognizing and dismantling harmful tropes about transgender and other marginalized leaders, we take steps toward building institutions where everyone's contributions are valued. When leadership embraces diversity as a core strength, it becomes a powerful force for transformation.

I also invested in my own development. When Human Resources told me she didn't approve of my approach to leadership, I asked what trainings I could take, and I followed her recommendation by enrolling in "The Working Mind: Workplace Mental Health & Wellness." Leadership skills can be learned.

In my final two years as chair, my goal was to promote as many people in my department as I possibly could, while making sure the department as a whole developed the skills to support promotion cases. I wanted to invest in our collective development. I used my time to develop myself, my employees, and my department as a whole. This increased my influence and legacy.

Protect Glass Cliff Leaders

Be aware of any leader that may be in a Glass Cliff situation.

Do you have anyone in your organization who has just stepped into a complex role? Is this an inexperienced leader? Did they step into a leadership role when no one else would accept the offer? If so, ask what this new leader needs. Ask what their department needs. You may have to ask more than once because in their first weeks they may have no idea what they need. There may be some specific kinds of support that a department in crisis needs. The needs could be financial, but some supports come without a price tag, like clearer communication, compassion, and empathy.

An inexperienced leader in a complex situation is going to need support. They may need training, they may need to work more closely with their supervisor, and they would likely benefit from peer support as well. Can you offer support, development, mentorship, and specific suggestions? Can you use your leadership position to protect and develop this new leader? Some employees may be less aware of resources than you are. An employee whose parents are academics or lawyers might understand what their most effective strategies are when faced with hostility and bias. Another employee may need your help.

A Glass Cliff leader may need to ask for help, but asking for help and support requires psychological safety. If a Glass Cliff leader is put under great scrutiny, pressured to leave the position, and discouraged from seeking mentorship, they won't be able to ask questions. In my case, the backlash when I asked for clarity on a policy was such that I stopped asking. Any perceivable uncertainty could be documented as a failure of my leadership. I developed the strategy of having staff people make queries about policy without mentioning me.

In a leadership role, when you are asked to hold an employee accountable, consider the context. Who is controlling the narrative? What incentives are impacting the person who is bringing the complaint? Is your employee experiencing marginalization? Are they members of intersecting marginalized groups? Historically marginalized people are vulnerable to biases that emerge in one person and are spread among others. Members of marginalized groups are forgiven for imperfections less easily and are more likely to be criticized and punished for errors (Schiller et al., 2014). Members of marginalized groups may have a particular vulnerability to public humiliation. The internet is cruel and impossible to control, so any public criticism you offer can be amplified. Marginalized leaders, especially Glass Cliff leaders, face disproportionate scrutiny and risk. To be clear, I'm not suggesting that criticisms of a Glass Cliff leader could never be informative. I'm suggesting curiosity and a constructive approach.

You can ask yourself: Do we do this with other employees? When I received the secret report suggesting that I be replaced as chair, one of the complaints about me was that our department's self-study document was "signed off by the Chair." It didn't mention that the same document also bore the signature of two cisgender people: the dean and a vice provost. No one recommended that those cisgender people be removed from their positions. It was recommended that I be replaced. This contrast was remarkably obvious. Someone should have noticed the difference in treatment. If your actions are extraordinary, you should get curious to understand why. Effective leadership requires contextual awareness and a commitment to psychological safety.

Protect Your People

When you are a leader, there is nothing more important than the well-being, safety, and productivity of your people.

Keeping people in my department safe meant managing with compassion and calling people in rather than calling them out. During the course of my term, I was instructed by the dean, by a journalist, and even by the university's Ombudsman to hold department members accountable when actions or communications had offended someone. I could have responded in ways that were disruptive to productivity and harmful to my employees' sense of self, but I chose a different path. In each case, I had a conversation with the employee in question, calling them in, not out. I asked them about their values, their intention, and their impact. I invited them to contemplate how things might unfold differently in the future. Notice that leading with care isn't weakness. I still addressed the concerns that were brought forward and collaboratively created solutions.

When the Inquiry and Remedy Committee learned what had happened to lead to an explosion of claims, they knew that they had to do what they could to make the university a safer place for students, staff, and faculty. They led our department's participation in conversations about the reform of policies. They committed to making sure the university's administration understood what had transpired. Most impactfully, they advocated for the investigation that led to the Flaherty Report and followed up with the administration to make sure Flaherty's recommendations were being implemented. They cared about our people and wanted to keep our people safe.

In addition to guarding safety and well-being, a leader is in a position to protect productivity. There came a time when I needed to let people know that it was okay to get back to work. Once the Quillette article was published and the Flaherty investigation was underway, I let people off the hook. I described our progress at a departmental faculty meeting and told people that the work we needed to do together as a department was done. And to the best of my ability, I protected them from further intrusions and interruptions.

Policy and Poise: Tools for Surviving Institutional Bias

Queer and trans leaders may need to rely on procedural clarity and emotional discipline to withstand institutional pressure.

When The Administrator was trying multiple approaches to remove me from office, I called an employment lawyer. "What does your contract say?" was the first thing he asked me. We reviewed the contract and realized that there was no termination clause. The university doesn't have any policy or procedure for removing a chair from office. The Administrator's only strategy was to bully me until I voluntarily stepped down. I decided to weather the storm. Knowing that I couldn't actually be removed as chair allowed me to refocus my attention on my work.

If you find yourself threatened at work, consult your policies. If necessary, consult a lawyer who understands the issue at hand. Knowing your options allows you to make the best decisions possible and may actually allow you to sidestep the issue and refocus your attention to your impactful work.

Document everything.

I have notes from my meetings with The Supervisor and The Administrator, and of course I have kept all of their emails and the letters they have sent. Document everything when you find yourself under the gun. The more adversarial the relationship, the more extensive the notes need to be.

Guard your emotions.

I survived a meeting with The Administrator, Human Resources, and the Director of Human Rights. My strategy was to remain polite, and when I was asked for my response at the end of the meeting, I said I had nothing to add. They were creating an emotionally intense situation and any reaction would have been noted. Once they have harmed you, it is going to be difficult for them to believe that you didn't deserve it. The Just World Fallacy describes how their instincts are telling them that you got what you deserved (Lerner & Miller, 1978). Cognitive dissonance theory posits that it is stressful to hold beliefs that contradict one's own behavior (Festinger, 1959). The more they have done to harm you, the more they are invested in believing that you are a bad person so that you deserve what they have done to you. During the series of disciplinary meetings I endured, there was nothing I could say that would not be interpreted as insubordinate, cagey, or disrespectful. Any response would justify how I was being treated. If your employer believes that you are a bad person, any outburst (or perceived outburst) will confirm their belief. Your best strategy is to keep doing good work.

Take someone with you to meetings. This ally can serve as a witness, take notes, give you some perspective, and help you keep your emotions under control.

One of the queer superpowers that Fram and Cavallaro describe is that queer and trans folks have had to work hard to learn how to define themselves (Fram & Cavallaro, 2024). I've been called names in the streets. I've been called names in school, and now The Administrator has told my colleagues that I harm students. These accusations have an impact, but I know I am not a monster. I get to define myself. I know that, like my cisgender colleagues, I am fallible and I am doing my best. The fact that I had practice defining myself in the face of discrimination, vulgarities, and legal threats helped me reorient to my own self-definition during my term as chair. When my university's legal team wrote, "Regrettably, Dr. Rutherford did not (and has not) lead." I didn't let them define my leadership. I reminded myself that the work I was doing was important. When I became department chair, I was answering a calling. The importance of that work hadn't changed.

Keep Showing Up

As department chair, I frequently reminded my colleagues to "Keep showing up."

I wanted our department members to feel brave enough to participate in university governance and to show up for networking so that people would know us. Persistent visibility is both a form of resistance and a strategy for change.

After The Administrator tried several approaches to remove me from my position, all without showing any curiosity about who I was as a person or who I was as a leader, I felt deeply misunderstood. As with my department as a whole, I personally needed to resist the urge to feel shamed by what was being said about me. I needed to keep showing up.

In the years since The Administrator's attempts to remove me, I've responded to a lot of invitations to campus events. I've attended presentations delivered by my research colleagues from departments all over campus. I've attended senate meetings when topics on the agenda were of interest to me. I attended the provost's holiday party and the president's retirement reception. I was able to employ crucible experiences like harassment and coming out to stay grounded and courageous.

Don't retreat in shame.

It is not always easy for transgender people to keep showing up. Sarah McBride, U.S. House Representative from Delaware and the nation's first openly transgender member of Congress, said:

> When the work you're doing every single day is so directly about who you are as an individual and who you are as a person, it can be both exhausting and empowering in different moments.
>
> *(McBride, 2018)*

There are a lot of university administrators who have never worked closely with a transgender leader. Even if the discomfort is mostly unconscious, it can impact the support and development of transgender leaders. Mere exposure can break down barriers and reduce prejudice (Flores et al., 2018), so as a transgender leader, one of the most important things I can do to put people at ease with transgender colleagues is to be there. By showing up in spaces that may not yet understand or welcome me, I allow people to get to know a trans guy, I foster inclusion, and I model courage. I've had trans and non-binary students and faculty tell me that I have been a meaningful role model.

Beyond my university, I need to be visible as a transgender leader. I need to be the one who tells my story, and I need to be the one who describes what I have experienced. I have been invited to tell my story as the first transgender department chair at conferences, at churches, and in other academic departments. My being visible as a role model can impact trans people who are considering leadership. Telling my story can help other leaders prepare their organizations for their first transgender leader. A lot of the transphobia out there is rooted in inexperience. Defeating transphobia will rely on trans people showing up persistently.

I'm using my own story as an example, but this lesson is not unique to me. Whoever you are, you can show up as well, but never feel an obligation to use your identity to educate others in your workplace. You need to practice self-care and make sure that you are choosing when you have the capacity to be present for the learning of others. Their learning about your identity is ultimately their work to do, not your responsibility.

Create Relationships and Strategic Networks

Anyone in a leadership position needs a network of mentors, leaders, and friends in high places.

My job as chair was not only to lead my department but also to advocate for it and to serve as the liaison between my department and the rest of the university. I needed connections with multiple groups on campus. In order to support your people, you'll need such connections too. Networking is not optional.

Before I became chair, I was pretty quiet. Because I trusted the upper administration at my university, I didn't go to general faculty meetings. I had never been to a senate meeting. Board of governors meetings were completely foreign to me. But once I became chair, I realized that I really needed to start building relationships across campus. I needed to meet people in different faculties and in the central administration. I made lots of coffee dates and lunch dates with department chairs and leaders across campus. I reached out to people who were new to campus. I began using social media to connect with people.

By the time The Administrator was hiring an external law firm to investigate me, I had friends across campus including in the upper administration. Many people offered to intervene. Some offered to speak directly to The Administrator on my behalf. Having friends in lots of different places on campus kept me from being gaslit because I had a perspective on conversations that were happening about me at the highest levels of the university.

Fram and Cavallaro identify networking as one of the queer superpowers. Trans and queer folks need to find allies who will be there for them in times of adversity. I had allies both on campus and in the local queer community, and I intentionally cultivated the queer community on campus. I knew I was going to need help. I underestimated how important my network was going to be.

Apologize Like a Boss

My first opportunity to apologize came even before I was chair, while I was serving on the search committee that was looking for the next department chair. The dean was having a difficult time filling the role, and some of my colleagues had suggested that I should be the next chair. As I delivered this suggestion to the committee, I made the impromptu remark "You're not going to like this ... " In my mind, I was acknowledging that there were procedural challenges—I could not become the next chair while I was serving on the search committee. The dean thought I was suggesting that she didn't like me and was offended. She interrupted the meeting to say so. As soon as she let the committee know that I had offended her, I apologized immediately. My instincts told me that I had to jump in, clarify what I meant, and diffuse the situation. The meeting proceeded.

An apology is one of the most powerful tools in your toolbox. Some people are slow to apologize because admitting that you are imperfect stings. Some people are wary of apologizing because their lawyers have advised them not to. They don't want to incur liability. An apology is a repair overture that fosters trust, defuses conflict, and prevents costly fallout. It is not a sign of weakness.

Apologies are an underutilized leadership tool. In the town where Melanie and I live, we experienced some violence at our pride celebration in 2019. In the aftermath, there was a lot of commentary about who was to blame, some of it centering around whether the local police and the city itself had been prepared to defend those gathered at pride against violence. In the days that followed, the mayor met with leaders of the local queer community, including Melanie, who asked for a public apology. The mayor objected: it wasn't his fault, it wasn't his doing, and he wasn't even there. Over the course of a very constructive meeting, Melanie explained that because he was the mayor, the buck stopped with him. Despite the fact that he hadn't been there or been in charge of organizing security for the event, an apology from him would be meaningful. The meeting ended with a draft of an apology, which was finalized and made public later that day. His apology allowed the community's anger to subside sooner than it otherwise would have. Sometimes leaders can make use of an apology, even in situations that were not really their fault.

In the wake of the events of 2020 that impacted our department, we have never heard an apology from the administration. We never heard the words "I'm sorry." Our dean told me within weeks of my becoming chair that our department would not receive an apology from the upper administration for the disruption to our department. In March of 2023, the dean attended a department meeting and told us that she felt "sorry for how difficult it has been for us," but she didn't say she was sorry. I knew that they were going to have a hard time repairing the relationship and rebuilding trust without an apology.

Apologies save money. Is it ironic that lawyers will often advise leaders to avoid apologizing? The university has spent hundreds of thousands of dollars in legal fees and restitutions following the crisis in our department. If they had apologized and repaired relationships immediately, these costs would likely have been substantially less. Maybe it is not ironic that lawyers discourage apologies; the profits from the fallout are tremendous.

Apologize early. Apologize easily. Apologize more than you really have to.

Be Approachable

During my term as chair, I was profoundly misunderstood by my superiors, and I asked myself what I could have done to help them understand me better. For introverts, cultivating approachability and mastering the art of "managing up" are essential skills.

One lesson that I have personally taken to heart is that I need to make sure that I am approachable. Toward the end of my term, The Supervisor went on an administrative leave and I was reporting to a new boss. We worked very well together, we both were intentional about creating a relationship, and he worked with me to support my department. We got along so well that Melanie and I invited him and his partner over for dinner. We both agreed that we had had a good year, but he told me that when he first met me, he didn't know how to read me. He said he could not tell what I was thinking during conversations with me.

I've been told that before. When I was lecturing on a regular basis, I sometimes heard that students found me unapproachable. When I became chair, I was aware that I needed and wanted to be more approachable. I didn't want to be inscrutable. Melanie told me that in order to appear more friendly, I either needed to wear interesting shoes, as a conversation starter, or I needed to have facial expressions. I own a lot of shoes now.

Before I became chair, I didn't know anything about "managing up," a term that refers to managing your relationship with your boss. It includes letting them know about your job-related accomplishments and also includes understanding their goals and priorities so that you can support their success. I was not in the habit of telling my boss about my work but I soon learned that some people were particularly good at managing up. They frequently contacted me to ensure I knew what a great job they were doing. I also learned that there was a cost to not managing up.

My failure to manage up contributed to the strain in my relationship with The Supervisor. I talked to her about the fact that I was quiet. I acknowledged that my quietness created an opportunity for people to misunderstand me. She agreed. She expressed that she wished she knew more about me and more about what was happening in my department. My journey taught me that silence can be misread and that being approachable is a form of care.

Step Up, Step Back

Inclusive leaders create space for shared vision and shared values. This becomes essential in times of trouble.

In my Unitarian Universalist community, the launch of a new group often includes the creation of a new covenant, specifying how that group will be together. Usually someone will nominate "step up, step back" as a constructive practice. Stepping up means participating in the group. Offer your thoughts when you are moved to do so or when someone asks you to. Stepping back means giving space for someone else to voice their thoughts. "Step up, step back" means creating a balance in the group between your own participation and that of others.

In leadership, the principle is the same, but the balance is different. A group will need more and expect more stepping up from their leader. As chair, it was up to me to convene meetings, create agendas, and assign committee work. It was up to me to create processes and decide what topics we would discuss in depth at faculty retreats.

At the same time, I wasn't leading alone. Creating shared leadership involved me making space for the influence of others. Creating a strategic plan involved creating space for the vision that everyone, students, staff, and faculty, had for the department. Navigating our department's relationship with the upper administration required me to listen carefully to the thoughts and feelings of people in the department.

Obviously, a leader has to step up. A leader also needs to know when to step back and let others participate. An inclusive leader can use their influence to help bring forward the voices of those who are marginalized. This balance transforms leadership from authority into collaboration.

Find What Sustains You

During times of trouble, we need to care for ourselves.

I had to find a way to get through the darkest period of my career. Self-care is important for everyone and especially important when we are navigating difficulties. I belong to a gym where I work out pretty intensely three times a week. None of the shenanigans that I experienced at work disrupted this commitment. I eat a fairly healthy, balanced diet based on whole foods. Throughout the trials of my leadership, I was able to maintain my physical health.

I also made a point to involve myself in activities that would distract my mind. Before my children left for university, I would come home from work everyday, put on some music, and cook dinner. It usually took an hour or so. For me, this was a catharsis, and a way to distract myself from what was happening to me at work.

I tended to my social connections throughout this period. I attended my local Unitarian Universalist church religiously. I stayed connected to friends through dinner dates, theater, and sporting events. In the early days, a lot of socializing took place outdoors on hikes through the nearby forested areas. All of these practices were important to my health and therefore supported me in getting my job done.

In a leadership position, our priority is to care for the people we serve, but we can't do that without caring for ourselves. You won't be helping anyone if you end up on a stress leave. Caring for yourself, for your body, and for your mind requires some planning and a commitment. When it seems like you don't have time for self-care, that may be when you need it most. Self-care is not indulgent but essential.

Return on Investment: The Value of Transgender Leadership

The resistance I met to my inclusive approach to leadership, involving shared leadership and consensus decision-making, was not unique to me. Dr. Raquel Willis, a renowned transgender activist and writer, believes, "When trans people lead, we challenge the status quo—not just in policy or representation, but in how power and belonging are understood. That challenge is what makes us threatening to some, but transformative for many." I hear my own journey reflected in Willis's insight.

When The Administrator shared with me the message she had received from a faculty member in another department (expressing shock over my attempts to reintegrate my colleagues and asking that I be removed as chair), she asked me if I was surprised. The message was surprising because I believed that I was succeeding in my position and because I knew that I had my colleagues' support, but it was not surprising that someone out there wanted me to be removed. I had been the object of homophobia and transphobia before, and I knew what it felt like.

The premise of Fram and Cavallaro's book *Forging Queer Leaders* is that queer and trans folks have unique leadership skills because of the adversity and marginalization they have faced, not in spite of it. The book's title points specifically to the resilience that trans people have in the workplace. Trans folks can be tough, and if you attack them, it is not likely to be the first time they have been attacked (Fram & Cavallaro, 2024).

Trans folks have an ability to appreciate multiple perspectives.

People who have transitioned are people who have moved through the world being perceived as women and also moved through the world being perceived as men. That is a rare opportunity when it comes to points of view. Shortly after I transitioned, I was attending a conference, and a group of new colleagues took me out to a restaurant in Philadelphia. As the evening wore on, each one left for home. I was alone in a part of town I didn't know. My first thought was to catch a taxi back to my hotel, but no taxis were circulating in the neighborhood. I walked alone for an hour through an unfamiliar city in the dark of night. I was a bit nervous, but I was also aware that I might be having a very different experience if I hadn't transitioned. I was perceived as a man, and no one gave me any trouble. I was able to appreciate two points of view as I navigated the sleepy, yet potentially dangerous, city. In the case of conflict, trans folks can often serve as the bridge between perspectives.

Throughout my term, I knew I had broad support not just because of the anonymous survey but because faculty, staff, and students told me how much they appreciated my leadership style. Stepping into this complex role, I felt certain that I was well positioned to listen to various viewpoints, and my colleagues trusted me to do the work of listening. In my case, the fact that I was a transgender leader was useful because the women in the department trusted me and the men in the department trusted me. The false narrative that trans leaders "exclude" others or are "not inclusive of women" ignores the labor of engagement and empathy that is often invisible but essential.

Transgender people bring empathy to leadership. Queer and trans folks are adept at reading the room—assessing what allies and what threats might be present—and we are adept at code-switching—adapting language and cultural norms depending on who is in the room. In addition, trans folks have insight into the experiences of marginalized people.

Trans folks are pretty likely to understand human rights laws, to know their rights and the rights of their employees, and to know where to go for help when there are workplace challenges. I have been fighting for social justice all my life. I've sued the province and won. This was not my first rodeo.

It is likely that trans leaders have a network of queer and trans wisdom and resources. When transphobia arises in the workplace, we usually have trusted allies that have seen solutions to such challenges before. My attempts to build bridges—through extensive consultations, open dialogues, and collaborative strategic planning—were sometimes misunderstood. Instead of being seen as efforts to weave a more inclusive collaboration, they were weaponized to question my integrity and leadership readiness.

It is not enough to expect marginalized leaders to "prove" their worth through resilience or exceptionalism. Institutions must actively dismantle the tropes and biases that erode trust in diverse leadership. The easy part is creating policies that protect trans leaders from discrimination and harassment. The hard part is cultivating a culture that has the competence to make space for transgender leadership. For transgender people to gain access to leadership, we need more than superficial inclusion. This will involve a profound reimagining of leadership itself. To truly support trans leadership, institutions must move beyond token inclusion and commit to fostering psychological safety and reimagining leadership. Making space for transgender leadership may transform our understanding of leadership, but it will be worth it.

Respond Compassionately to Misgendering

Misgendering should be handled compassionately.

Every organization needs to have the conversation about misgendering so that people know how to respond when it happens. When I mentioned to Human Resources that I had been misgendered at a meeting she had attended, she responded by signing an attestation saying that I had not been misgendered, thus documenting that I lied about being misgendered. Universities need to foster compassionate, informed responses to misgendering by validating lived experiences and creating respectful repair practices that affirm the dignity of transgender employees.

First, let's start by recognizing that misgendering is a sensitive issue. When I hear someone using a feminine pronoun (she, her, or herself) to refer to me, I always find it jarring. It isn't just surprising; it is a gut punch. It will take me a second to regroup and circle back to the conversation at hand. In some cases, misgendering can actually expose someone's gender history. The emotional impact of misgendering can be amplified if it is intentional, persistent, and meant to cause harm. If an employee reports to you that they have been misgendered, first check in with them, see if they are okay, and check whether they are prepared to continue with the conversation.

Second, changing meetings to remote and recorded is never an appropriate response to an employee being misgendered. Creating a situation where a transgender person cannot be in the same room with other employees is very othering. It makes it appear that the trans person is so monstrous that people cannot be in the same room as them. Recording only meetings that include a transgender employee is also othering. It creates the appearance that the employee has done something wrong. This should never have been suggested.

Don't believe everything you hear. Or don't hear. The fact that Human Resources signed an attestation saying that I was not misgendered suggests that she didn't hear it when it happened. She may not have a lot of experience with transgender people or with people being misgendered. If you want to admit that you didn't hear the misgendering, that is your prerogative. Deciding that, because you didn't hear it, it must not have happened is an unwarranted inference.

This situation would have been even worse for me if there had not been a witness who heard the misgendering. I might have been left to question my own perceptions. Am I being irrational? Am I paranoid? Did I hear what I thought I heard? I would have been vulnerable to gaslighting. Gaslighting is cruel.

When I teach my queer etiquette class, I have some simple rules for repair if you've accidentally used the wrong pronoun or name. If everyone in the conversation is aware of the trans person's gender history, correct yourself and apologize quickly, then move on. Don't dwell on your apology, and don't make it about you. If there are some people in the conversation who don't know the gender history of the person you've misgendered, then just move on without bringing attention to the slip. You can apologize later in private.

Calibrate Your Vulnerability

I've heard the advice that, as a leader, I need to show that I'm vulnerable. Leaders are advised to tell our own stories. We should be personal, authentic, and vulnerable. This advice is meant to make a leader more relatable, more human, and more approachable. But the advice is tailored for the cisgender white leader who would otherwise be seen as living a life free of struggle. While vulnerability is often championed as a leadership strength, the expectation to disclose personal struggles is not universally safe or empowering. This advice, if taken up by leaders of vulnerable groups, plays out differently.

We are making space in leadership for lots of people, including leaders who are queer or transgender, who have mental health diagnoses, who come from an economically challenging background, or whose ethnic or religious community doesn't look like their peers at work. To what extent are these leaders expected to expose their own vulnerability? To what extent is any employee expected to disclose the ways in which their background is unlike their peers? Who does this disclosure serve? I've been wondering if the advice that leaders are supposed to bring their vulnerability to work is actually universal. Vulnerability can compromise authority.

Yes, leaders should attempt to be relatable and accessible. But plan ahead. Make sure you have allies who have the skill and the authority to help you if you lose control of a situation. A leader from a vulnerable group may need some guardrails.

The Fragility of Good Faith

With the election of Donald Trump, we started hearing people express surprise at his power. Can he do that? Can the president create barriers to voting? Can he dismiss the inspectors general who ensure ethics in federal governance? Can he end birthright citizenship? Can he redefine gender?

We were raised to believe that the federal government had built-in checks and balances, but we were learning that the collaborative administration of the government actually relies on good faith. I learned that good faith is required in the governance of most institutions. When that trust erodes, marginalized individuals are left without recourse.

My university, like most universities, has processes that an employee can rely on for help if they encounter hostility at work. Those processes may not be helpful in changing the behaviors of people who hold the highest positions in the institution because everyone at the top knows each other and the possibility of independent assessment evaporates.

When I filed a complaint the week that I experienced profanity in a supervisory meeting and The Supervisor told me "I'm tired of you," I was unable to find anyone in the university who had enough power to help me. The person whose job it was to assess my claim was The Supervisor's supervisor, who supported her "100%." I was not given the new reporting structure I had asked for, instead I was told that I was "not to circumvent or avoid communication with [The Supervisor]," and I was offered a year's leave if I stepped down.

Because of a lack of good faith and a lack of independence among the president and vice presidents at the university, I had no safe place to seek support. Most institutions don't contemplate creating guardrails that would disrupt a high-ranking official's attempt to act on their implicit biases, from transphobia to cronyism. They are expected to have no implicit biases. This is a vulnerability, to marginalized employees and to the institution.

Growing Edges

A friend who read an early draft of this book asked, "Did you ever try anything that didn't work?" Sure I did. Most of my efforts were successful because people in my department trusted me. They were going to support my efforts and buy into my strategies for repair. But not everything got done. The five-year strategic plan that we all worked so collaboratively on and that upset The Administrator so much was never fully executed. There are good ideas in the document about engaging with policymakers to try to influence policy. We said we wanted to collaborate with science museums to bring demonstrations and experiments to the public. We achieved a lot of the goals we set for ourselves. We invested in leadership development, we embedded our values into our culture, we built bridges between research laboratories, and we showed up for university governance. But some of our aspirations never became a priority.

Personally, my biggest growth opportunity was managing up. I didn't do a good job of telling my boss the great work I was doing, and I didn't understand that I was supposed to be telling her. When I told Melanie that I had been invited to reflect on anything that didn't work, she said, "Everything you did was extremely successful, except that you ruined your chance for promotion and ruined your career."

References

Festinger, L. (1959). *A theory of cognitive dissonance*. Stanford University Press.

Flores, A. R., Haider-Markel, D. P., Lewis, D. C., Miller, P. R., Tadlock, B. L., & Taylor, J. K. (2018). Challenged expectations: Mere exposure effects on attitudes about transgender people and rights. *Political Psychology, 39*(1), 197–216. https://doi.org/10.1111/pops.12402

Fram, B., & Cavallaro, E. (2024). *Forging Queer leaders: How the LGBTQIA+ community creates impact from adversity*. Jessica Kingsley Publishers.

Lerner, M. J., & Miller, D. T. (1978). Just world research and the attribution process: Looking back and ahead. *Psychological Bulletin, 85*(5), 1030–1051. https://doi.org/10.1037/0033-2909.85.5.1030

McBride, S. (2018). *Tomorrow will be different: Love, loss, and the fight for trans equality*. Crown Archetype.

Schiller, B., Baumgartner, T., & Knoch, D. (2014). Intergroup bias in third-party punishment stems from both ingroup favoritism and outgroup discrimination. *Evolution and Human Behavior, 35*(3), 169–175. https://doi.org/10.1016/j.evolhumbehav.2013.12.006

11

How I Survived the Glass Cliff

When I took the role of chair, I was due for a sabbatical, but I delayed it because I thought the department needed stability in its leadership. Despite all that I went through, I was able to complete my five-year term and honor the commitment I had made. Following my term as chair, I will take my delayed sabbatical and start a new line of research on the experiences of transgender leaders in academia.

The scrutiny and harassment I experienced took a toll on me. There were moments of despair. There were sleepless nights. The repeated meetings attended by Human Resources were demotivating. For many months, I experienced irresistible rumination as I tried to figure out what was happening and why. What was being said about me behind closed doors? Knowing a bit about how I was being treated by The Supervisor and The Administrator, some people asked me how I kept going. Maybe you are wondering why I didn't just quit? Was it sheer tenacity? Or was it stubbornness? People have been curious about how I held myself together considering the scrutiny I was under, the hostile meetings, and the repeated attempts to replace me. What got me through those five years was knowing I wasn't alone. I had support, and I had people who believed in me.

Leaders need to know when and how to ask for help and to recognize we can't go it alone. George Odell wrote, "We need one another when we are in trouble and afraid. We need one another when we would accomplish some great purpose, and cannot do it alone. We need one another in the hour of success, when we look for someone to share our triumphs. All our lives we are in need, and others are in need of us" (Odell, 1993, p. 468).

I am grateful to my family and to my UU community for anchoring my values and providing perspective and emotional support. I would not have been able to remain chair if I had not had the complete and unreserved support of the academic colleagues in my department and in my faculty association. I had transgender allies in the community who had experience navigating the legal processes designed to protect all of us against discrimination and harassment. I had colleagues who work in DEI spaces who provided advice and perspective.

Family

I began this book by telling the story of my family heading out of the driveway so my kids could keep up their swim practices by temporarily moving to New Mexico. I was completely isolated for three and a half months during COVID-19-related shutdowns. Well, eventually, my wife and kids came home and my family has been a tremendous source of support while I've survived my term as my department's first transgender department chair.

As I weathered the onslaught, Melanie was my rock every single day. Right alongside me, she has survived years of me being attacked by my employer. She listened to me everyday as I described the unfathomable meetings, letters, and emails. She's been supportive of my staying in my job and also supportive as I've pondered job opportunities elsewhere. Melanie is a leadership coach with a leadership book of her own, and she was interested in watching me develop my leadership skills. She wants me to succeed, and she's willing to go where we need to go for me to find success. But being my steadfast supporter was not easy for Melanie. She later told me that she was deeply troubled by the fact that she wasn't able to protect me from The Supervisor and The Administrator.

During the worst of it, I would come home from work everyday and Melanie would ask "Did they try to kill you today?" She later tried to describe what it was like for her to see me get through that period. "It felt like whiplash," she told me. "One day you would come home and talk about how much people in the department appreciated you, trusted you, and constantly thanked you. The next day I would hear another story about The Supervisor or The Administrator putting together their case against you." To say that she found my journey confusing and disorienting is an understatement.

She told me how powerless she felt when I'd sit in the living room with her in the evenings after dinner. "When I asked about work, it was like opening up a faucet. There was no way to stop the flow," she said. "It was like having a trauma client who wouldn't leave my office and there was no way to finish the session." She knew she was the primary person I talked to about what I was experiencing at work, so she never tried to stop me from sharing, but she felt that she had no way to get away from it and no way to save me from it. That period tested her resilience. There was no way of knowing what might come next.

In the evening after The Administrator first offered me a leave if I would resign as chair, Melanie came with me to the home of a colleague where some of my colleagues had gathered to try to understand why The Administrator had turned on me and how the department should respond. Melanie was tearful as she described her disappointment in the university. Previously, we had loved the university. When we decided to move so I could take the job, we believed we would be here for my whole career. We were friends with a former president who served for 15 years. It was a deep disappointment to see the culture of the university changing under new leadership.

Melanie believed in my approach to leadership, and she believed the university would benefit from giving me more leadership opportunities. She was concerned about how The Administrator's portrayal of me might impact my professional reputation and my prospects of advancing in leadership. She understood the events of that day as a sign that I would never have greater leadership opportunities in my current institution.

As a professional coach, Melanie coached me through this experience and encouraged me to further my own coaching training so that I would have other career options if the university was unable to create a psychologically safe workplace for me. She helped me craft my email response to Human Resources and spent hours helping me write my application to the Human Rights Tribunal.

My mom Janice has always been one of my biggest supporters. I frequently call her in the evening and tell her what is going on at work. She's been horrified at how I have been treated. Lately, she's been marching every week in the streets of Eugene, Oregon, carrying homemade signs that read "Trans lives matter," and "NO to Scapegoating Trans People." Knowing how much my church has served as a haven for me during these hard times, she recently made a substantial donation to my church.

She is a professor herself, and I often send drafts of emails, talks, or essays for edits. As a mom, she was of course all in for providing emotional support no matter how difficult my tribulations. Also, as a mom, she found it difficult to read about some of The Supervisor's and The Administrator's treatment of me. It is good to have your mom in your corner.

My kids are queer advocates. They've attended pride parades since they were in a stroller, and they are better at updating people's names and pronouns than anyone I know. I did not share all of the details of my journey with my children, but kids know when there is trouble in the household. They know that I have been under a tremendous amount of stress at work over the last few years. I've been less available to them than I used to be. They've noticed it, and they've been very tolerant of my preoccupation. They have been supportive of the fact that there were times I had to prioritize my work over my family life. One day when I had a friend of mine over, working at the dining room table to write a summary of everything that had been going on at the university, my son Emerson walked through the room and said, "Good luck with whatever you are working on there." I appreciated the support.

My Unitarian Universalist Community

My UU community has been important to my experience as a transgender leader in many ways. When I was blindsided by the administration undermining me in the local newspaper in the summer of 2021, I was away for the weekend in the forest at Unicamp, a nearby spiritual retreat center and summer camp owned and operated by a number of UU congregations. The trip was planned, but also turned out to be well-timed. That weekend and many times since as I've struggled in my role as a transgender leader, the Unicamp community was my lifeline. I was able to sit with and talk to sympathetic people. I had enjoyed a great career at my university for 20 years, but with the change in leadership in the upper administration, things changed. The Administrator did not know me, had never met me in person, and was saying terrible things about me. People in my community, on the other hand, shared my values. They knew me and believed in me.

At Unicamp, I found solace. People listened compassionately and offered care and concern. Those conversations at Unicamp served as a buffer against gaslighting. My employer was publicly impugning my inclusivity and my values, which were central to my leadership and to my very identity. I don't know what it would have felt like if I hadn't had my UU community, but I likely would have started to doubt myself—to believe that, despite my weeks of consultation and outreach, I had not been inclusive enough.

The goal of Unicamp is to provide a safe and welcoming space, and for me it did. The 50 acres include forest, beaches, caves, and a magnificent hilltop called Cowpye Hill with stunning views of the neighboring landscape.

I also benefited from being part of the Interfaith Working Group at my university, which allowed me to strengthen my connection with the pastoral resources on campus. This allowed me to find a place for my UU perspective on campus and to receive support from members of the group.

There were also several times during my first years in office that I benefited from pastoral conversations with the university's ecumenical chaplain. I went to their tiny cinder block-walled office in the student center, poured a cup of tea, and, in the quiet of their office, we would light a candle before our conversation began in order to mark the intention of the time we spent in discussion.

I told the chaplain about the state of my department and how I was trying to create a space for healing. I shared that I had been called to the position. I talked a lot about how I was being treated by The Supervisor and The Administrator. The chaplain observed that I did not have psychological safety in the workplace and that I would need to have this safety in order to get my work done.

When I felt conflict, emotion, and chaos, I would begin to question whether I was living my values. These conversations were an opportunity to reaffirm my values and make sure my decisions and actions were aligned with them.

These conversations were a source of solace. I am grateful to the chaplain for helping to ease my mind and give me peace.

One of the advantages of being part of a religious or spiritual community is pastoral care. During the worst of it, Melanie suggested I meet with my minister about how I was struggling. I think she needed me to have someone else to talk to. My minister listened, asked questions, and reflected. She offered compassion. We didn't really talk about any strategy or response and that was okay. The value of her pastoral care came from my experience of being seen, heard, and understood. She reflected both how being misgendered can cause distress for a transgender person and how the university's response was impacting me.

My Colleagues

Members of my department were also tremendously supportive, including my predecessor. Department chairs who serve a full five-year term earn a one-year administrative leave, during which they have no work obligations. In an incredibly selfless act, my predecessor postponed his leave for a year to assist me in dealing with the department's turmoil. The department was deep in crisis and I was a rookie. He knew I was going to need his support.

When The Administrator offered me a paid leave if I resigned, I immediately called my predecessor. He helped me speculate about why I was being asked to resign—maybe the university administration was embarrassed by the public narrative around the department I was leading, he offered. Maybe they were trying to sweep the whole debacle under the rug, and I was frustrating them because I kept trying to talk to them about it. He told me often administrators at such a high level don't know what is really going on within various departments. He said the conversation with The Administrator didn't mean I wasn't doing a good job, and he advised me not to step down.

Following that meeting with The Administrator, I needed to consult with members of my department to learn if they wanted me to continue to be chair and to see if anyone else in the department thought we would be better off with a different chair. Within days, one of our department's associate chairs called a meeting of all of the faculty except me. All of the faculty members showed up to discuss whether they wanted me to step down. The associate chair who convened and facilitated the meeting reported to me that people were clear that they wanted me to remain—provided that I felt strong enough to do so. Knowing that faculty members in my department had full confidence in me and were willing to support me in the face of The Administrator's attempts to remove me gave me the boost I needed to stay on.

Many people in my department wrote to me individually. These letters acknowledged the unique set of challenges that I stepped into when I became chair. They mentioned the stability and calm that they felt since I became chair. They relayed that, since I became chair, they had been able to redirect their focus to research and teaching. One colleague commented on how much calmer the department felt since I became chair. One colleague said that my leadership style was dignified.

I heard, "All of us agree that you have been doing a fantastic job as a chair." Some appreciated my investment in leadership development. They commented on my commitment to creating a welcoming and inclusive environment. They observed that consensus decision-making allows them more time to collect their thoughts and gather their nerves to speak up. They offered personal words of encouragement: "I hope you are holding up ok." They acknowledged that "It has not been an easy ride." They expressed being saddened by The Administrator's treatment of me. They expressed gratitude. They encouraged me to continue leading. Their support was heartwarming. I had done my best to help them through a difficult time, and their support of me meant the world. I was grateful for these notes. They gave me the strength to continue.

The Gang of Four spoke directly to The Administrator when she engaged a law firm that conducts "Workplace Investigations." Although The Administrator never told me that she had called off the workplace investigation, my four senior colleagues appear to have convinced her that such an investigation would be destructive. The Administrator is a tremendously powerful person on campus, so resisting any of her initiatives is dangerous. I was impressed with my colleagues' thoughtful and constructive communication that was both diplomatic and unwaveringly clear. They wanted The Administrator to give me a chance at being a successful leader, and they said so. The support of these four very senior faculty members meant the world to me. I don't know how I would have weathered this attempt to remove me from my position without their leadership.

When I received a summary of the secret report from Human Resources, recommending that I be replaced as chair, once again, members of my department had my back. A colleague of mine knew one of the two external reviewers. He asked her whether she had heard any concerns about my leadership from within the department. She said, "Absolutely not." Another colleague spoke to another reviewer at a conference, and she said she had not contributed to the secret report. She felt she and the other reviewers had been used, and she didn't want to volunteer for our university in the future. This networking confirmed that negative rumors about me had not originated within my department. My colleagues had my back.

As chair, I gave my all to the people in my department, and it was heartening to see that they would go to the ends of the earth for me as well. I would not and could not have continued as chair if my colleagues hadn't been so supportive.

Throughout my term as chair, my faculty association offered support, guidance, advocacy, and resources. They sent a representative with me during meetings with

The Administrator and Human Resources so I wouldn't have to face them alone. And when it was decided that meetings with me had to be online and recorded after I was misgendered, the president of our faculty association spoke to The Administrator. She made it clear that the faculty association would support me because it was in the best interest of the faculty association to have a workplace that was safe for transgender faculty members. It is the role of the faculty association to advocate for the working conditions of faculty members, and I appreciated their support.

Transgender Allies

While I was serving as chair, there were transgender colleagues who provided support. One of them, a transman who has a leadership position in academia at another university, shared helpful advice about how I could navigate discrimination and harassment. He encouraged me to see if there was a way to repair the relationships with The Supervisor and The Administrator since their support would be integral to my success at work. As my supervision had changed during my time as chair, I have been careful to cultivate positive relationships with those who supervise me.

Another trans colleague, a public school teacher who has also had issues in the workplace since transitioning, was also a source of wisdom and comfort. They had experienced gender-related harassment, discrimination, and intimidation at work and had trouble getting their union to take the matter seriously. This friend was very familiar with the process of bringing human rights complaints forward.

When I told them about the secret report that came out of our academic review and about the workplace investigation that was being planned regarding my leadership, they reviewed all the documents I had been given by my employer and reinforced for me how my human rights should be protected at work, including that my gender specifically should be grounds for protection. They told me that being cut off from communication with the university's DEI office because I had filed a complaint was reprisal and should not be allowed. It was helpful to hear that the way I was being treated was not appropriate and to hear that I had rights.

Leaders in Inclusion

After I filed a complaint and was subsequently misgendered, I was no longer allowed to talk to my friends and allies in the DEI office, which was an incredible blow because the DEI office would normally be an important resource for a transgender employee who is being treated unfairly. In a university context, staff can be more vulnerable to disciplinary actions than a professor, especially a professor like me who is tenured, so I didn't push it when my friends in that office told me they couldn't talk to me anymore. Once we were forbidden to speak to each other, I didn't reach out to them again.

However, there were other people I could talk to, people who were not in the DEI office. When The Administrator was trying to persuade me to step down from my position, one of the reasons she gave me was that our department's five-year strategic plan didn't "center Indigenous ways of knowing and being." I immediately made an appointment with the associate dean of equity, diversity, inclusion, and indigeneity. I told her that The Administrator wanted to replace me, and I told her about the comment about our strategic plan. I asked her advice.

Our strategic plan clearly stated that "We will explore informing and blending western with Indigenous forms of knowledge" in the section that discusses our approach to undergraduate teaching. In our community outreach section, we discussed our intention to collaborate with local Indigenous groups and invite Indigenous students to do research in our labs. We said that we wanted to create internships for Indigenous students. We wanted to hold knowledge-sharing exercises to better understand how science and Indigenous knowledge enhance each other. In the section about research, we described projects that would incorporate nearby Indigenous groups and incorporate their traditions in our study of the psychology of music. I asked the associate dean if we should have pulled those comments out of the sections and instead written one section dedicated to Indigenous ways of knowing and being. She thought integrating Indigeneity into our regular activities was a better approach. I asked if there was a template, an example, or any guidelines for including Indigeneity into strategic plans. There was not.

I also reached out to an Indigenous colleague of mine. She is a member of local Indigenous groups and, as a good friend of mine, is often available for a chat. I told her what The Administrator had said about our strategic plan not centering Indigenous ways of knowing and being. I also shared that our recent reviewers suggested that I be replaced because I was using formal consensus decision-making in my department. The irony is that consensus is fundamental to the local Haudenosaunee leadership and governance, as it is to many Indigenous cultures across North America. The Administrator's comment about Indigenous ways of knowing and being juxtaposed with the idea that I should be removed for supporting consensus decision-making brought out a chuckle.

She told me that it was not really the place for a white administrator to decide whether my leadership was consistent with Indigenous ways. She posited that my department's strategic plan probably did not center Indigenous ways of knowing and being any less, or more, than other department's strategic plans. More fundamentally, she shared that the incorporation of Indigenous ways wasn't a requirement that should be used to discipline or remove a leader from their position. She thought the incorporation of Indigenous wisdom should be a conversation opener.

We should collaborate to imagine how and when to use Indigenous ways in our teaching, research, and leadership.

I would go on long walks at the local cemetery with another friend, a former member of the DEI office. She is such a kind person; she never said no to an invitation for a walk. We walked on cool spring days and hot summer days. She would inquire about how I was doing and I always had some new stories to tell. She would express dismay about how I was being treated. Human Resources, who documented each of my disciplinary meetings, was well-known to my friend so she was aghast at the stories I told about how I was being treated. Because she knew many of the people involved, she was able to offer reflections and advice.

She is a strong feminist and was able to advise me early in my term when I was figuring out how to communicate with my frightened department. She no longer had any sway on campus, but her steadfast support and availability helped me navigate my confusion and distress over how deeply misunderstood I was by The Supervisor and The Administrator. I was lucky to have her as an ally.

Without the support of all these people, I would have been left to wonder if maybe there was something wrong with me. Did I deserve this treatment? Or did everyone get treated like this behind closed doors? All of these conversations were a buffer against gaslighting and reassured me that the way I was being treated was not how most chairs are treated. My treatment was extraordinary.

Counseling

As I started to open up to people about what had happened to me, the most common reaction was disbelief. The second most common reaction was to ask me if I was getting counseling. I finally am, but it took me years to get myself to a therapist.

While I was going through the worst of it, I was still the leader of the department. I thought that, as a leader, I needed to be strong and I needed to appear unflappable. Most of the people in my department did not know how badly I was being treated, even while they were aware that The Administrator wanted to replace me. I was careful not to bring that trauma to others at work. I wanted to shield my colleagues and make sure they stayed focused on their academic work. In order to be effective, I thought I always had to appear ready to lead. I didn't think I could be available to people who had questions and challenges if I revealed the stress I felt from being attacked from above. I would literally go into the office and tell people "Everything is under control." Rather than opening up and talking about my feelings with a counselor, I kept my mask on.

A larger barrier to accessing emotional support was the fact that the counseling that was available to me through work was organized by the university's human resources office. If I even logged into the portal, the human resources office would know. I read the fine print carefully, where I learned that notes taken during a session with me could be subpoenaed. Knowing that I was under intense scrutiny made it difficult for me to navigate even the initial online intake form for counseling.

About halfway through my term, as we were settling the grievances, the university's lawyer had asked me to hand over my medical records. As one of a very few transgender employees on campus, I thought this request was invasive and I ended up paying a lawyer out of pocket to resist this request. With the help of my lawyer, I was able to rebuff this request, and I did not have to give my employer my medical records.

At the online portal for our employee counseling services, I managed to answer the intake questions but then found that there was an intake evaluation that took place online, to see if I really needed counseling. I was chatting in a chat window of the portal, unsure if I was talking to a person or a bot. They asked why I wanted to talk to a counselor. I said, "workplace stress." That was not enough to get me an appointment. They asked me to disclose more about what was happening at work. I froze. I recalled that the university's lawyer had threatened me with a lawsuit if I told anyone the reasons I had filed a claim against The Supervisor. I recalled that Human Resources managed this whole service, was keeping my file, and had said that I was lying about being misgendered. I disconnected from the chat and closed the portal.

Eventually, in my final year of my term as chair, I managed to make it through the intake and made an appointment with a counselor. In our first conversation, I told him the highlights of my harrowing journey, and he confirmed that it was unusual to be treated the way I had been treated. The more people I share my story with, the more difficult it is for my employer to gaslight me.

My Own Resilience

Fram and Cavallaro posit that the adversity we face both in and out of the workplace drives skill development. Such experiences prepare transgender leaders

> to listen and respond better to criticism, articulate their own points of view, even in the face of opposition, create strong support systems, advocate for themselves and others within systems of power and privilege, examine their own desires, needs, and life goals, and take care of themselves psychologically, physically, and materially.
>
> *(Fram & Cavallaro, 2024. p. 43)*

This quote resonates with me and my experience. If I hadn't weathered homophobia and transphobia before, The Administrator's treatment of me would have been utterly perplexing. The fact that I examined my own goals and values as I stepped into the role anchored my acts and my decisions. I worked hard to create a strong support system as soon as I became chair, and I owe my survival to this support system. The idea that trans folks may be prepared to advocate for themselves and others within systems of power and privilege helps explain why I was able to survive in my role as chair.

In my response to the secret report that Human Resources sent to me, I wrote, "Leading this embattled department has required me to draw on strength I never knew I had and never imagined I would need." The strength I found in myself is the strength that Fram and Cavallaro describe as being forged in a crucible.

I learned that I am strong, and I am resilient. But a transgender leader should be able to experience leadership without having to be constantly on guard. I should have had the opportunity to develop in leadership, making mistakes and asking questions, just like anyone does when they experience leadership for the first time.

Détente

Because of the support of my family, my UU community, my department, my faculty association, and transgender allies, I was able to survive the Glass Cliff appointment until a détente was finally negotiated between my department and the upper administration.

During the last two years of my term, I reported to supportive supervisors after I was finally given a new reporting structure. They were the support I needed. One told me, "I know that you are really good at the mentoring piece and the supporting piece." He commented that my "prioritizing shared leadership and leadership development was apparent." He recognized my mentorship of junior faculty members. He acknowledged the healing that my leadership has facilitated and encouraged me to continue. Having a supervisor that I could partner with made leading easier and made my work more effective. Finally, I could ask questions or ask for support when I'm stymied.

In my fourth year of serving as chair, The Supervisor went on a year-long leave, and in her absence, a colleague served in her role and acted as my boss for a year. He arrived determined to create a better relationship with my department. I was pleased that this was his priority and was eager to have a better relationship both between me and my supervisor and between my department and the upper administration. I'll admit that I initially thought he was naive. I, too, had come into my role thinking that I would be able to repair our department's relationship with the university's administration. Surely all we needed to do was sit down together and we would be able to rebuild our relationship based on our common values. I had found this fantasy bridge-building impossible, but years had passed, and maybe he was right that we had an opportunity to mend.

He talked to the president and the provost of the university and made a pitch for support for our department. He suggested that we might need some material support, such as new faculty hires. Moreover, he pressed them hard for a public statement retracting their prior characterization of our department and for a visit to the department to mend fences. When The Supervisor had shown me her finger, a summary of the Inquiry and Remedy Committee's findings was sitting on her table. One of the points in that summary was "To this date, there has been no attempt by the Administration to correct the narrative for the university community." That was about to change.

My new supervisor was successful in persuading the president and the provost that it was time for such a correction, and on December 13, 2024, the university issued a statement in the university's newspaper. The president said, "I realize that the last several years have been an extremely challenging and uncertain time for members of the department and have been particularly harrowing for those against whom unsubstantiated allegations were made." He drew attention to recommendations made by the Flaherty Report and said that some of those recommendations were being implemented. "Our ongoing goal is to ensure that our policies are fair and equitable to all members of our community. It is by regularly reviewing our processes and responding to thoughtful critique and feedback that we make positive improvements for the benefit of all," he wrote, going on to say that we were "focusing on the outstanding research and teaching that the department's members have long been known for." This statement was a relief for me and other faculty members. The university was ready to acknowledge what a difficult time we had had. They seemed prepared to participate in our repair.

Even more meaningful was the fact that the president and provost scheduled a meeting to visit our department to listen to our perspective. As the meeting approached, I told my mentor Gail that this was time for me to really lead with intention. I organized four planning meetings for the department ahead of the visit. We talked about what we needed to communicate. We talked about the trajectory of the meeting—we wanted to convey the depths of everything we had been through but we also wanted to end on a hopeful note. We even strategized about the room setup. We let the president and provost sit closest to the door so that they would feel comfortable while they were with us. We started the meeting with planned opening words and a planned speaker order, and each speaker had their remarks written and prepared ahead of time.

We met at 10:30 a.m. on a Wednesday in late December. I stood and watched out of our second-floor meeting room as the president and provost crossed the long central courtyard to our building, accompanied by the president's chief of staff. As soon as they were close to the building, I hurried down to the front door and welcomed them. This was the first time the president had been in the building since our crisis began. The fact that both the president and the provost came to see us was monumental, clearly signaling a change in their view of us.

I started with an opening statement, which included the line, "Today we come together to do the hard work of community. This work is difficult and takes time. We do this work because our department is important to us, our university is important to us, and the people in our community are important to us." For fifty-five minutes the president and provost sat wordlessly and listened as members of our department read impact statements. People spoke from the heart. People cried. Even though emotions were palpable, it was a slow and contemplative meeting.

When it was my turn, I told them, "We want to partner with you in making our university a safer place to work and learn. As a first step, we would like you to open a line of communication so that our department can be involved in the implementation of the recommendations from the Flaherty Report. Not only would such a collaboration make our university a safer place to work and learn, but the collaboration itself could serve as the foundation of the trust we are rebuilding between our department and the upper administration."

I'm sure their lawyers were still not allowing them to apologize to us, but both the president and provost said that they never wanted anything like this to happen again. After the president and provost had a chance to speak, I closed the meeting with these comments: "What has been done cannot be undone. But I want us to be clear that we have agency. We know what an inclusive and caring community we have been and what a productive academic department we have been. Now it is up to us to create our path forward."

With the exception of a few planned vacations, I had spent everyday of my term as chair working in my office, working where people could find me. On that day, after people in my department finally got to tell their story, after we got as close to an apology as we would ever get, I went home in the middle of the day. I went to bed and slept until morning.

References

Fram, B., & Cavallaro, E. (2024). *Forging Queer leaders: How the LGBTQIA+Community creates impact from adversity*. Jessica Kingsley Publishers.

Odell, G. E. (1993). We need one another (Reading no. 468). In Unitarian Universalist Association (Ed.), *Singing the living tradition* (p. 580). Unitarian Universalist Association.

Acknowledgments

A single-authored book is not a solo endeavor. I appreciate all who have helped me on this project. Leadership coach Gail Rappolt was the first to help me with this book, working with me to describe my values, my leadership strategies, and my approach to working with a department in crisis. Together we created the first version of a book proposal. Next I worked with the award-winning journalist and writing coach Anne Bokma, who helped me shape my value-based leadership into a narrative. Melanie Parish, Master Certified Coach and Advanced Certified Team Coach, provided feedback on the book multiple times, including when it was a jumble of ideas. Janice Rutherford, PhD, provided feedback and edited the first complete draft. I was gifted with extensive feedback on later drafts from Pat Dickenson, EdD, Stephanie Ounpuu, PhD, and Bill Johnston, former editor of the Hamilton Spectator. Sela Solomon read a late draft and provided comments. Thank you all!

Index